New book releases are free the first 48 hours. Every month, there is a free download on Kindle. To know of new releases and dates for free downloads, please subscribe at

www.TessaCason.com

Tessa Cason
5694 Mission Ctr. Rd. #602-213
San Diego, CA. 92108
www.TessaCason.com
Tessa@TessaCason.com

LEGAL NOTICE AND DISCLAIMER:

From author and publisher: The information in this book is not intended to diagnose or treat any particular disease and/or condition. Nothing contained herein is meant to replace qualified medical or psychological advice and/or services. The author and publisher do not assume responsibility for how the reader chooses to apply the techniques herein. Use of the information is at the reader's discretion and discernment. The author and publisher specifically disclaim any and all liability arising directly or indirectly from the use or application contained in this book.

Nothing contained in this book is to be considered medical advice for any specific situation. This information is not intended as a substitute for the advice or medical care of a Physician prior to taking any personal action with respect to the information contained in this book. This book and all of its contents are intended for educational and informational purpose only. The information in this book is believed to be reliable, but is presented without guaranty or warranty.

By reading further, you agree to release the author and publisher from any damages or injury associated with your use of the material in this book.

All Thing EFT Tapping Manual

Emotional Freedom Technique

Tessa Cason, MA

My EFT Tapping Story

I established a life coaching practice in 1996 when life coaching was in its infancy. After several years, I realized that desire, exploration, and awareness did not equate to change and transformation for my clients.

Exploring the underlying cause of their pain, knowing their motivation to change, and defining who they wanted to become, did not create the changes in their lives they desired.

My livelihood was depended on the success of my clients. I realized I needed a tool or technique or method to aid my clients in their quest for change.

At the time, I knew that everything in our lives, all of our thoughts and feelings, choices and decisions, habits and experiences, actions and reactions were the result of our beliefs.

I knew that the beliefs were "stored" in our subconscious mind.

I knew that to transform and change our lives, we needed to heal the underlying unhealthy, dysfunctional beliefs on the subconscious level. I needed a tool, technique, or method to eliminate and heal the beliefs stored in the subconscious mind.

I visited a friend who managed a bookstore and told her of my dilemma, that I needed something to help my clients truly change and transform their lives. She reached for a book on the counter, near the register. "People have been raving about this book on EFT, Emotional Freedom Technique. Try it and see if it can help your clients."

In the 1990s, the internet was not an everyday part of our lives. Popular books sold more by word of mouth than any other means. Managing a bookstore, my friend knew what worked and what did not work. I trusted my friend, so I purchased the book.

As I read the book and discovered that EFT was tapping our head, I was unsure if this was the technique that would help my clients. I had some adventurous and forgiving clients whom I taught how to tap. When **every single client** returned for their next appointment and shared how different their lives had been that week because of tapping, I took notice! I was intrigued.

I learned that the first statement we needed to tap was: "It's not okay or safe for my life to change."

I learned that clearing an emotional memory was different from clearing beliefs.

I learned that tapping one side of the body was more effective that tapping both sides simultaneously.

I learned that when a tapping statement did not clear, it meant there were other dysfunctional beliefs preventing the statement from clearing. When a statement didn't clear, I turned the statement into a question.

I learned that for EFT Tapping to work, we needed to find the cause of an issue.

Have you heard the joke about the drunk looking for his keys under a street lamp? A policeman asks the man what he is looking for. "My keys," says the drunk. The policeman joins in the search. Not finding the keys, the policeman asks the drunk if this is where he lost his keys.

"No, I lost them in the park."

Confused, the policeman says, "Why are you looking here and not over there?"

The drunk answers, "The light is brighter here."

EFT Tapping is a simple and effective tool to heal our issues when we address the cause and not just the symptoms. Addressing the symptoms would be looking for the keys under the street light. The symptoms are easily identified. But, healing the symptoms does not heal the underlying cause.

I learned we are complex, complicated beings wrapped up with a lot of history, traumas, dramas, and experiences. Sometimes finding the cause is like walking through a maze...there are a lot of dead ends, turns, and wanderings.

Clients started asking for tapping homework. I wrote out statements for them to tap. Soon, I had a library of tapping statements on different emotional issues.

I have been an EFT Practitioner since 2000. Working with hundreds of clients, one-on-one, I learned how to successfully utilize EFT so my clients could grow and transform their lives.

TABLE OF CONTENTS

How to Approach This Manual

There is no specific suggested order when reading this book. The book begins with information about EFT Tapping followed by two EFT Tapping stories. Pete's story was included to follow his journey to discovering his bottom line to healing. In Katherine, Megan, and Beau's story, each had to learn how to deal with an obnoxious person.

Moving forward in our lives requires healing our disappointments and regrets. The final section provides examples of how to use EFT Tapping and scripts to heal our disappointments and regrets.

Chapter 1
EFT Tapping – Emotional Freedom Technique

EFT Tapping is a very easy technique to learn. It involves making a statement as we contact the body by either circling or tapping.

An EFT Tapping Statement has three parts:

Part 1: starts with "**Even though**" followed by

Part 2: a statement which could be the **dysfunctional emotion or belief**, and

Part 3: ends with "**I totally and completely accept myself.**"

A complete statement would be, "**Even though I fear change, I totally and completely accept myself.**"

Instruction for the Short Form of EFT Tapping

The instructions below are for using the right hand. Reverse the directions to tap using the left hand. It is more effective, when we tap, to tap only one side rather than both.

I. SET UP – BEGIN WITH CIRCLING OR TAPPING THE SIDE OF THE HAND:

A. With the fingertips of the right hand, find a tender spot below the left collar bone. Once the tender spot is identified, press firmly on the spot, moving the fingertips in a circular motion toward the left shoulder, toward the outside, clockwise. Tapping the side of the hand can also be used instead of the circling.

B. As the fingers circle and press against the tender spot or tap the side of the hand, repeat the tapping statement three times: "Even though,___[tapping statement]___, I totally and completely accept myself." An example would be: "Even though I fear change, I totally and completely accept myself."

Side of the hand

Tender spot below the left collar bone

©Tessa Cason, 2022.

3

II. TAPPING:

A. After the third time, tap the following eight points, repeating the [tapping statement] at each point. Tap each point five – ten times:

    1. The inner edge of the eyebrow, just above the eye. [I fear change.]

    2. Temple, just to the side of the eye. [I fear change.]

    3. Just below the eye (on the cheekbone). [I fear change.]

    4. Under the nose. [I fear change.]

    5. Under the lips. [I fear change.]

    6. Under the knob of the collar bone. [I fear change.]

    7. Three inches under the arm pit. [I fear change.]

    8. Top back of the head. [I fear change.]

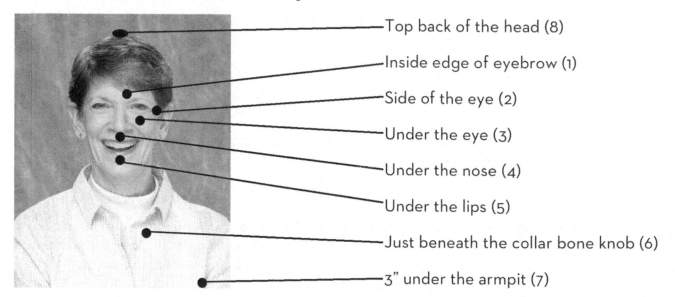

Top back of the head (8)
Inside edge of eyebrow (1)
Side of the eye (2)
Under the eye (3)
Under the nose (4)
Under the lips (5)
Just beneath the collar bone knob (6)
3" under the armpit (7)

B. After tapping, take a deep breath. If you are not able to take a deep, full, satisfying breath, do eye rolls.

III. EYE ROLLS

A. With one hand tap continuously on the **back** of the other hand between the fourth and fifth fingers.

B. Hold your head straight forward, eyes looking straight down.

C. For six seconds, roll your eyes from the floor straight up toward the ceiling while repeating the tapping statement. Keep the head straight forward, only moving the eyes.

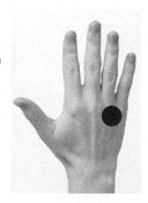

IV. TAKE ANOTHER DEEP BREATH.

Chapter 2
EFT Tapping, Beliefs, and the Subconscious Mind

EFT – Emotional Freedom Technique

EFT is a technique that allows us to change dysfunctional beliefs and emotions on a subconscious level. It involves making a statement while tapping different points along meridian paths.

The general principle behind EFT is that the cause of all negative emotions is a disruption in the body's energy system. By tapping on locations where several different meridians flow, we can release unproductive memories, emotions, and beliefs that cause the blockages.

A Belief is...

A belief is a mental acceptance of, and conviction in, the Truth, actuality, or validity of something. It is what we believe to be true, whether it is Truth or not. A belief is a thought that influences energy all the time.

A Dysfunctional Belief is...

A dysfunctional belief is a belief that takes us away from peace, love, joy, stability, acceptance, and harmony. It causes us to feel stressed, fearful, anxious, and/or insecure.

The Conscious Mind is...

The conscious mind is the part of us that thinks, passes judgments, makes decisions, remembers, analyzes, has desires, and communicates with others. It is responsible for logic and reasoning, understanding and comprehension. The mind determines our actions, feelings, thoughts, judgments, and decisions **based on beliefs.**

The Subconscious Mind is...

The subconscious is the part of the mind responsible for all our involuntary actions like our heartbeat and breathing rate. It does not evaluate, make decisions, or pass judgment. It just is. It does not determine if something is "right" or "wrong."

The subconscious is much like the software of a computer. On the computer keyboard, if we press the key for the letter "a," we will see the letter "a" on the screen, even though we may have wanted to see "t." Just as a computer can only do what it has been programmed to do, we can only do as we are programmed to do.

Our programming is determined by our beliefs. Beliefs and memories are "stored" in the subconscious.

THREE RULES OF THE SUBCONSCIOUS MIND

Three rules of the subconscious mind include:

1. Personal. It only understands "I," "me," "myself." First-person.

2. Positive. The subconscious does not hear the word "no." When you say, "I am not going to eat that piece of cake," the subconscious mind hears, "Yummm! Cake! I am going to eat a piece of that cake!"

3. Present time. Time does not exist for the subconscious. The only time it knows is "now," present time. "I'm going to start my diet tomorrow." "Tomorrow" never comes; thus, the diet never starts.

Beliefs precede all of our thoughts, feelings, decisions, choices, actions, reactions, and experiences...

Our beliefs and memories are stored in the subconscious mind.

If we want to make changes in our lives, we have to change the programming, the dysfunctional beliefs in the subconscious.

Three rules of the Subconscious Mind:
Personal
Positive
Present time

Chapter 3
How Does EFT Tapping Work?

1. Acceptance: The last part of the tapping statement, we say, "I totally and completely accept myself." **Acceptance brings us into present time.** We can only heal if we are in present time.

2. Addresses the current dysfunctional beliefs on a subconscious level: To make changes in our lives, we have to change the dysfunctional beliefs on a subconscious level. The middle part of the tapping statements are the "instructions" for the subconscious. **To make changes in our lives, we only care what the subconscious hears.**

3. Pattern interrupt: Dysfunctional memories and/or beliefs block energy from flowing freely along the meridians. Tapping is a pattern interrupt that disrupts the flow of energy to allow our **body's own Infinite Wisdom to come forth for healing.** (Tapping both sides does not act as a pattern interrupt.)

4. Mis-direct: One role of the physical body is to protect us. When our hand is too close to a flame, our body automatically pulls our hand back to safety. An EFT Tapping statement that agrees with the current belief is more effective. The physical body is less likely to sabotage the tapping if it agrees with the current belief.

For the EFT Taping statement "I fear change":

* This statement appeases the physical body since it agrees with the current belief.
* The tapping disrupts the energy flow so our Truth can come forth.

The body will always gravitate to health, wealth, and well-being when the conditions allow it. EFT Tapping weeds the garden so the blossoms can bloom more easily and effortlessly.

Chapter 4
Benefits of Using EFT Tapping

* The last part of the statement is, "I totally and completely **accept** myself." **Acceptance** brings us into present time. Healing can only take place when we are in present time.

* By tapping, we are **calling forth our Truths**. The keyword here is "**our**." Not anyone else's. If my name is "Lucas," tapping the statement "Even though my name is Troy," my name will not change to Troy.

* Tapping **calls forth our body's Infinite Wisdom.** When we cut our finger, our body knows how to heal the cut itself. Once the dysfunctional emotions, experiences, and beliefs have been "deleted," our body **automatically** gravitates to health, wealth, wisdom, peace, love, joy...

* By changing dysfunctional beliefs and emotions on a subconscious level, the changes we make with EFT are **permanent.**

* EFT Tapping can change:

Beliefs
Emotions
Self-images
Our story
Thoughts
Mind chatter
Painful memories

* EFT Tapping can neutralize stored memories that block energy along the meridians.

* EFT Tapping can desensitize emotions. We might have a difficult person in our life who ignores us and/or criticizes us, so we tap the statement: "This difficult person [or their name] ignores and criticizes me."

Tapping does not mean they will no longer ignore and/or criticize us; however, it can **desensitize us,** so we are no longer affected by their behavior. Once we have desensitized the emotions, our perception and mental thinking improve. We are better able to make informed decisions. We don't take and make everything personal. Our health is not negatively impacted. Our heart doesn't beat 100 beats/minute. Smoke stops coming out of our ears, and our faces don't turn red with anger and frustration.

Chapter 5
What We Say As We Tap Is VERY Important!

All of our beliefs are programmed into our subconscious minds. If we want to change our lives, we have to delete the dysfunctional beliefs on a subconscious level. The statements we make as we tap are the instructions for the subconscious mind.

THE TAPPING STATEMENTS WE WAY AS WE ARE TAPPING ARE CRITICAL FOR THIS TO HAPPEN!

Example: You get in a taxi. Several hours later, you still have not arrived at your destination. "*Why?*" you ask. Because you did not give the destination to the taxi driver!

Tapping without saying an adequate tapping statement is like riding in a cab without giving the cab driver our destination!

For EFT Tapping to be MOST EFFECTIVE the Tapping Statement is CRITICAL!

EFT Tapping allows us to delete the dysfunctional beliefs on a subconscious level. The statements we make as we tap are instructions to the subconscious mind so our Truth can come forth.

Chapter 6
Using a Negative EFT Tapping Statement

Our beliefs **precede** all of our thoughts, feelings, decisions, choices, actions, reactions, and experiences.

If we want to make changes in our lives, we have to change the dysfunctional beliefs. Our beliefs are stored in the subconscious.

To change our lives, to change a belief, we only care what the subconscious hears when we tap. The subconscious does not hear the word "no." When we say, "I am not going to eat that piece of cake," the subconscious hears, "Yummm, cake!"

Example, if we don't believe we have what it takes to be successful and we tap the statement, "I have what it takes to be successful," the body could sabotage the tapping. We could tap and it won't clear.

Instead, if the statement we make is, "I do not have what it takes to be successful," the **"not"** appeases the physical body and the subconscious hears, "I have what it takes to be successful!"

A tapping statement with the word "no" or "not" works best!

Chapter 7
EFT Tapping Statements Are Most Effective When They Agree With Current Beliefs

The EFT Tapping statement is **more successful when** it **is something the body currently believes.**

The body is less likely to sabotage an EFT Tapping statement that agrees with the current belief.

One role of the physical body is to protect us from harm. (For example, if our hand gets too close to a flame, our body will pull our hand back to safety.) The body is less likely to sabotage the statement and the process if the EFT Tapping statement agrees with the current belief. Thus, it appeases the physical body.

For example, if our desire is prosperity and wealth and we tap the statement, "I am prosperous now," the body could sabotage the tapping by forgetting what we were saying, getting easily distracted, or our mind chatter may remind us we are not prosperous. We could tap and the statement, most likely, will not clear.

If the statement we say is "I am not prosperous now," the "**not**" appeases the physical body, and the subconscious hears, "I am prosperous now!"

Chapter 8
The Very First EFT Tapping Statement to Tap

The very first EFT Tapping statement I have clients and students tap is, "It is not okay or safe for my life to change." I have muscle tested this statement with more than a thousand people. Not one person tested strong that it was okay or safe for their life to change. (Muscle testing is a way in which we can converse with the body, bypassing the conscious mind.)

How effective can EFT or any
therapy be if it is not okay or safe
for our lives to change?

Since our lives are constantly changing, if it is not okay or safe for our lives to change, every time our lives change, it creates stress for the body. Stress creates another whole set of issues for ourselves, our lives, and our bodies.

Chapter 9
Tapping Both Sides or One Side?

Part of the effect of tapping is a "pattern interrupt" of the energy flowing along the meridian. When we tap on both sides at the same time, the effectiveness of the pattern interrupt is not as great.

I have found it more beneficial to tap only one side when tapping instead of two sides.

Chapter 10
Short Form or Long Form of EFT Tapping

The long form of EFT Tapping involves a sequence of tapping on the fingers, eye movements, humming, and counting.

After learning EFT Tapping, I utilized both forms to determine if one was more effective than the other. I wanted to determine if one was more effective in clearing beliefs, emotions, reframing, and/or for healing a story.

I FOUND THERE WAS NO DIFFERENCE.

Tapping the long form did not clear an issue that the short form did not clear. When an issue did not clear with the short form, we tapped the long form. The issue still persisted.

Since I could not discern an advantage to using the long form, I decided to use the short form to address more concerns of my clients in the time span of their sessions.

I also discovered that if a statement did not clear, other beliefs, issues, and/or emotions needed to be addressed before the resistant statement would clear.

Chapter 11
One Statement per Round of EFT vs
Multiple Statements per Round of EFT

Laser-focused Tapping vs Round Robin Tapping

Same Statement for all the Tapping Points in One Round
vs Multiple Statements in One Round of Tapping (Scripts)

Two styles of tapping for different purposes. One style is best for healing dysfunctional beliefs. The other style is best for healing emotions, desensitizing a story, situation, and/or memory.

I found that the laser-focused, one statement for a round of tapping was most effective for healing the beliefs. Multiple statements per round of tapping is great at healing emotions, desensitizing a story, situation, and/or memory.

SAME STATEMENT FOR ALL THE TAPPING POINTS IN ONE ROUND

After tapping the statement, "It's not okay for my life to change," and we are able to take a deep breath, we know the statement cleared. Then we tap, "I'm not ready for my life to change," and we are not able to take a deep breath, most likely, the statement did not clear.

Knowing the statement did not clear, we can focus on the reasons, excuses, and/or beliefs about not being ready to change our lives.

* Maybe the changes we need to make would require more of us than we want to give.
* Maybe we don't feel we have the abilities we would need if our life changed.
* Maybe we don't feel our support system, the people in our life, would support the changes we want to make.

Follow-up tapping statements for "I'm not ready for my life to change" could be:

* I do not have the abilities change would require.
* I am afraid of change.
* Others will not support the changes I want to make in my life.
* I am not able to make the changes I want to make.
* I do not have the courage that change would require.
* I am too old to change.

Tapping the same statement at all eight points is most effective for clearing beliefs. When a statement does not clear, we can focus on the reasons, excuses, and/or dysfunctional beliefs that blocked the statement from clearing.

Multiple Statements in One Round of Tapping (Scripts/Round Robin)

Tapping multiple statements in one round, also known as Scripts or Round Robin tapping, is excellent for healing a story, and desensitizing a memory or story.

Healing a broken heart, to desensitize the heartache of the break up, the following script/ statements could be said, one statement/point:

* My boyfriend broke up with me.
* I am heartbroken.
* He said he doesn't love me anymore.
* I do not know how I can go on without him.
* It hurts.
* I am sad he doesn't love me anymore.
* I am sad our relationship is over.
* I will never find anyone like him ever again.

Reframing:

Reframing is a Neuro Linguistic Programming (NLP) term. It is a way to view and experience emotions, situations, and/or behaviors in a more positive manner.

At the end of round robin tapping, we can introduce statements to "reframe" the situation.

An example of reframing could be:

* I want this chocolate.
* Maybe eating chocolate is wanting to reconnect to my childhood.
* Maybe eating sugar is a way of being loved.
* Maybe I can find a different way of being loved.

Round robin tapping, scripts, can desensitize the hurt and pain. It can heal the pain of our story. It may not rewrite the beliefs. To clear out the beliefs, it would be necessary to look at the reasons the relationship didn't work and why our heart is broken, or why we crave chocolate.

Round robin/script tapping can also be done by just tapping the side of the hand.

SIDE OF HAND TAPPING TO DESENSITIZE A STORY, SITUATION, AND/OR MEMORY

Just as in the round robin tapping/scripts, we said different statements, one after the other, we can say the same statements and just tap the side of the hand.

If a memory still "haunts" us, embarrasses us, and/or affects our actions in any way, this technique might be perfect to neutralize the memory.

For example:

As Sasha remembers the first dance she attended as a teen-ager, tears well up in her eyes. She starts to tap the side of the hand (SOH) as she tells her story:

My best friend, Samantha and I, were so excited about attending our first high school dance. We weren't old enough to drive so Sam's dad dropped us off in front of the high school auditorium where the dance was held.

(Continue to tap the SOH) We were in awe of how the auditorium was transformed into a palace. Sofas were placed around a hardwood dance floor in the center of the room. We promised each other we would be there for the other throughout the night so neither of us would be stranded alone.

(Continue to tap the SOH) Well, along came Billy McDaniels. Sam had had a crush on Billy since third grade. He asked her to dance and I never saw her again for the rest of the night.

(Continue to tap the SOH) Those three hours were probably the worst night of my entire life! No one asked me to dance. Every time I joined a group of girls, a new song would begin, and every one of them was asked to dance, everyone except me. I don't know why no one asked me to dance. I felt ugly, abandoned, and undesirable! Talk about being a wallflower. I thought I was invisible. I wanted to hide from embarrassment.

(Continue to tap the SOH) This was back in the days before cell phones. The auditorium didn't have a payphone to call my parents to come and get me. I had to endure three hours of humiliation watching every single girl be asked to dance EXCEPT me.

(Continue to tap the SOH) I never attended another high school dance again!

Whether we tap the side of the hand or the eight tapping points, the result is the same. Round robin tapping can desensitize emotions and memories very effectively.

There are different styles of EFT Tapping.
Find the style that works best for your desired result.

Chapter 12
Walking Backwards EFT (Backing Up)

As I was working with a client, they had an issue that was not clearing. Knowing that movement helps to clear issues, I decided to have the person stand up and walk backward. Literally, walk backward, step after step, facing forward while their feet moved backward.

Surprise, surprise, it worked. Every statement cleared as she backed up.

The next client came in. I had him walk backwards, and it worked with clearing issues for him as well. Both clients were somewhat athletic and did workout. I wanted to know if the Backing Up would work with non-athletic people. I was teaching an EFT class the next day. At the end of the class, we all backed up together. And, IT WORKED!

Let's say we want to process, "I will never be comfortable in the world." Stand up. Make sure nothing is behind you. Then walk backward while facing forward and say, "I will never be comfortable in the world. I will never be comfortable in the world. I will never be comfortable in the world. I will never be comfortable in the world." Repeat the phrase six - eight times.

When we back up, we say the same statement we would have made if we were tapping. We don't have to say the "Even though" or the last remainder phrase, "I totally and completely accept myself."

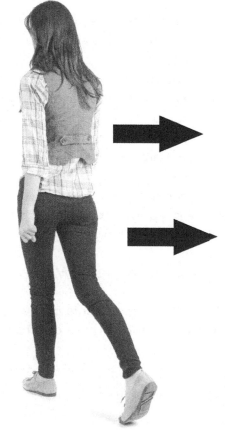

Walking forward represents forward movement in our lives. Walking backward represents the past.

Physical movement can help clear emotional issues and facilitate change.

Walking backward undoes the past and helps to clear, heal, and transform an issue in our lives.

©Tessa Cason, 2022.

Chapter 13
Intensity Level

One measure of knowing how much an issue has been resolved is to begin, before tapping, by giving the issue an intensity number (IL) between 1 and 10, with 10 being high.

For example, we want a romantic partnership, yet we haven't met "the one." Thinking about a romantic relationship happening, what is the likelihood, on a scale of 1 – 10, with 10 being very likely and 1, not likely at all, of a romantic relationship happening?

Okay. We give ourselves a 2. Now, let's start tapping!

When asked what the issues might be, "Well," we say, "it does not seem as if the people who I want, want me."

Great tapping statement. Tap, "Even though the people I want don't want me, I totally and completely accept myself." After tapping, we check in with ourselves; the IL has gone up to a 4, so it is now a little bit more likely.

What comes to mind now? "No one will find me desirable." Great tapping statement. "Even though no one will find me desirable, I totally and completely accept myself." Check the IL. How likely? 5. Cool! Progress.

What comes to mind now? "I'm not comfortable being vulnerable in romantic relationships." Great tapping statement. "Even though I'm not comfortable being vulnerable in a romantic relationship, I totally and completely accept myself." Check the IL. Now it is a 6. Still progress.

What comes to mind now? "Well, it feels like if I am in a relationship, I will lose a lot of my freedom." Make this into a tapping statement. "Even though I will lose my freedom when I am in a relationship, I totally and completely accept myself." The IL has gone up to a 7.

What comes to mind now? "Oh, if I was in a relationship, I would have to be accountable to someone!" Make this into a tapping statement: "Even though, I would have to be accountable to someone if I was in a relationship, I totally and completely accept myself." Wow...the IL is 9, very likely!

Giving an issue an Intensity Level gives at the beginning and throughout the session gives us an indication of the progress we are making with resolving and/or healing that issue in our lives.

©Tessa Cason, 2022.

Chapter 14
Yawning and Taking a Deep Breath

From Traditional Chinese Medicine, we know that when chi (energy) flows freely through the meridians, the body is healthy and balanced. Physical, mental, and/or emotional illness can result when the energy is blocked.

Dysfunctional beliefs and emotions produce blocks along the meridians, blocking energy from flowing freely in the body.

With EFT Tapping, as we tap, we release the blocks. As blocked energy is able to flow more freely, the body can now "breathe a sigh of relief." Yawning is that sigh of relief.

If, after tapping, we can take a complete, deep, full, and satisfying breath, we know that an EFT Tapping statement has cleared. This yawn is an indication that an EFT Tapping statement has cleared.

If the yawn or breath is not a full, deep breath then the statement did not clear completely.

Chapter 15
Integration...What Happens After Tapping

After tapping, our system needs some downtime for integration to take place. When the physical body and the mind are "idle," integration can take place.

Sometimes, in the first 24 hours after tapping, we might find ourselves vegging more than normal, sleeping more than normal, or more tired than normal. This downtime is needed to integrate the new changes.

After installing a new program into our computer, sometimes we have to reboot the computer (shut down and restart) for the new program to be integrated into the system.

After tapping, our bodies need to reboot. We need some downtime. When we sleep, the new changes are integrated.

HEALING BEGINS NATURALLY AFTER THE BODY HAS HAD A CHANCE TO INTEGRATE.

Sometimes, after tapping, we forget the intensity of our pain and think that feeling better had nothing to do with tapping. Something so simple could not possibly create the improvement in our state of mind!

When we cut our finger, once it is healed, we don't even remember cutting our finger. As we move toward health, wealth, and well-being, sometimes we don't remember how unhappy, restless, or isolated we once felt.

Chapter 16
EFT Tapping Doesn't Work for Me

Why might EFT Tapping not be working?

* The tapping statement might not be worded such that a dysfunctional belief and/or emotion is addressed and eliminated.
* The style (laser-focused style vs round robin) of tapping may not be effective for the statement to be cleared.
* The EFT Tapping statement is only addressing a symptom and **not the cause of the issue.**

FOR EFT TAPPING TO BE EFFECTIVE, THE CAUSE OF THE ISSUE NEEDS TO BE HEALED.

* Having an awareness of our issues does not heal the dysfunctional beliefs.
* Forgiving ourselves and/or someone else does not heal the dysfunctional beliefs.
* Talk therapy does not heal the dysfunctional beliefs.
* Desensitizing the emotions does not heal the dysfunctional beliefs.
* Healing the experience of a hurtful event does not change the dysfunctional beliefs.

EFT Tapping works best when

1) the statements are worded to eliminate the dysfunctional beliefs,
2) the most effective style of tapping is utilized, and
3) we are healing the cause, not just the symptoms.

Chapter 17
What to Do if an EFT Tapping Statement Does Not Clear

When a statement might not clear, turn the statement into a question. The statement, "It's not okay for me to be powerful," didn't clear. **Turn the tapping statement into a question:** "Why isn't it okay for me to be powerful?"

The answer might be:

* Powerful people are ruthless and heartless.
* I am afraid of being powerful.
* Being powerful would change me for the worse.
* Power corrupts.
* People would laugh at me if I tried being powerful.
* I would have to give up my fears and anxieties to be powerful.
* I might be called aggressive if I tried being powerful.
* I do not have the abilities, skills, or qualities to be powerful.
* Others would make fun of me if I tried being powerful.
* Powerful people are thoughtless and self-centered.

With these beliefs, it might not be okay or safe to be powerful or even explore the idea of being powerful. The statements above are tapping statements. Tap the answer to the question.

After tapping the answer to the question, revisit the original statement that did not clear. Most likely, it will now be cleared, and you will be able to take a full, deep, and complete breath.

Chapter 18
Do I Keep Tapping the Same Statement
Repeatedly if it Does Not Clear?

Tapping round after round after round, repeating the same statement over and over again as we tap does not ensure success.

Example: we tapped, "It is not okay or safe for me to be wealthy." It did not clear after one round of EFT Tapping. We truly want to be wealthy, so we continue to tap and tap the statement, and it does not clear.

What other beliefs might we have about money?

* It is not okay for me to have more than others.
* Others would think me arrogant and better than them if I had money.
* I do not know if people would be authentic with me or try to manipulate me for my money.
* My spending might go out of control, and I would end up with nothing.

With beliefs such as these, it might not be okay or safe to be wealthy. Rather than tapping round after round after round of the same statement, turn the statement into a question and tap the answers. "Well, why would it not be okay or safe for me to be wealthy?"

The answer you might discover is:

* I do not have the tools and skills to manage money.
* I have to work hard for my money.
* It is too much stress to maintain a wealthy lifestyle.
* The economy is too volatile and unpredictable. I might end up losing my wealth.

Once you uncover the additional beliefs and tap those statements, the previous statement(s) that did not clear, most likely will have cleared.

Our body is here to protect us. If having wealth would be harmful, then wealth will be kept at arm's length to protect us. It is important to heal the cause and not just the symptoms.

Chapter 19
I Tapped and I am Not Better. I Cleared This Issue and It Still Shows Up in My Life.

"I processed the issue I had, and I am not any better. Why?"

When we tap and process an issue, and the issue persists, it is not the process that did not work; it is the issue we processed. The correct CAUSE was not processed.

For instance, we resist change and often say, "I know I need to change, but..."

* Is our resistance to change, or do we lack something to move toward?
* We process being stuck in the past, but the real issue might be that we have nothing to move forward to in the future.
* Maybe it is about our lack of goals or not having the skills to fulfill a goal.
* Maybe it is our lack of dreams and believing this is the best it will ever be.

For instance, we may feel it is selfish to put ourselves and our needs first.

* Something bad will happen to those we love if we do not put them first.
* Others might call me selfish if I take care of my needs before theirs.

So, we process our selfishness. We process what others might say or think if we put ourselves first. Maybe the issue is not what others will think and say. Maybe the issue is us. Maybe we are just not that important to ourselves. Maybe the issue is self-love, self-respect, and self-worth.

> When we process, and the same issue
> persists, it is not the process that did not
> work; it is the issue we processed.

For example, our eating is out of control. So, we process this issue but our eating remains out of control. Maybe the issue is not about our eating being out of control.

* Maybe the issue is about stress or lack of self-confidence or anger, fear, and/or apathy that results in overeating.
* Maybe the issue is the lack of control we feel we have in our life.
* Maybe eating out of control is a symptom of our life is out of balance.

If we process and the issue seems to persist, look at the issue again, but from a different perspective. Flip it around. Look at it from the opposite perspective.

Process this new perspective.

* It might be about the future, not the past.
* It might be about our self-respect rather than someone else's respect for us.
* Maybe it is a symptom of another issue.

Flip it around.
Look at the issue from another perspective.

Chapter 20
Does a Negative Statement Parrot
My Negative Self-Talk?

A tapping statement with the word "no" or "not" may sound like our inner critic and/or our negative self-talk. Our inner critic and negative self-talk are actually our teachers. They are letting us know the dysfunctional beliefs we need to change to advance toward health, wealth, and well-being.

Since we ignore their words of wisdom, it seems as if our inner voice is critical and negative, as if they are nagging us. The truth is this: They are pointing out what needs to be healed in order for us to be healthy, wealthy, happy, and wise!

For example, let's say our negative talk goes something like this, "I will never lose the weight." What might the body be trying to tell us?

* Maybe the beliefs of being able to lose weight need to be examined and healed.

* Maybe if might be about being visible and present or dealing with the anger and shame beneath the weight or about our fear of intimacy and closeness.

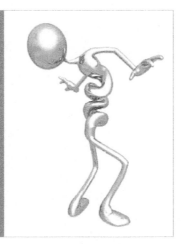

Our inner critic and negative self-talk are words of pearls shining a light on the path that needs to be healed.

Chapter 21
Can an EFT Tapping Statement Damage Me?

The body has an Infinite Wisdom. It will always gravitate toward health, peace, and joy. When we tap, we are calling forth our Truths, our Infinite Wisdom. EFT Tapping will not change our Truth. Gravity exists on Earth. Tapping will not change whether I would be affected by gravity or not.

Here's a simple example. My name is Tessa. If I tap the statement "Even though my name is Hannah," my name will not be changed to Hannah. It is not my Truth. The Infinite Wisdom of my body would not be affected by the statement, even if I tapped multiple rounds of EFT.

We cannot gravitate to health, peace, wealth, and joy if we are being prevented from doing so. "Blocked energy," or energy not able to flow freely in the body, prevents us from gravitating to wellness, prosperity, and happiness.

From Oriental medicine, we learn that when a person is healthy, energy moves through the body unobstructed. When the energy is blocked, illness occurs. With EFT Tapping, we are addressing the disruption and interruption in the flow of energy that keeps us from feeling healthy, wealthy, and powerful.

When energy can flow freely, unobstructed and our dysfunctional emotions and beliefs are removed, our Truth will move us toward health, wealth, and well-being.

Chapter 22
Science and EFT Tapping Research

EFT has been researched in more than ten countries by more than sixty investigators whose results have been published in more than twenty different peer-reviewed journals. Two leading researchers are Dawson Church, Ph.D. and David Feinstein, Ph.D.

Dr. Dawson Church, a leading expert on energy psychology and an EFT master, has gathered all the research information, and it can be found on this website: www.EFTUniverse.com.

TWO RESEARCH STUDIES

1) HARVARD MEDICAL SCHOOL STUDIES AND THE BRAIN'S STRESS RESPONSE

Studies at the Harvard Medical School reveal that stimulating the body's meridian points significantly reduces activity in a part of the brain called the amygdala.

The amygdala can be thought of as the body's alarm system. When the body is experiencing trauma or fear, the amygdala is triggered, and the body is flooded with cortisol, also known as the stress hormone. The stress response sets up an intricate chain reaction.

The studies showed that stimulating or tapping points along the meridians such as EFT Tapping, drastically reduced and/or eliminated the stress response and the resulting chain reaction.

2) DR. DAWSON CHURCH AND CORTISOL REDUCTION

Another significant study was conducted by Dr. Dawson Church. He studied the impact an hour's tapping session had on the cortisol levels of eighty-three subjects. He also measured the cortisol levels of people who received traditional talk therapy and those of a third group who received no treatment at all.

On average, for the eighty-three subjects who completed an hour tapping session, cortisol levels were reduced by 24%. Some subjects experienced a 50% reduction in cortisol levels.

The subjects who completed one hour of traditional talk therapy and those who had completed neither session did not experience any significant cortisol reduction.

Chapter 23
Is Lowering the Cortisol Level Enough to Permanently Change Our Lives?

Several things can lower our cortisol (stress hormone) levels including:
* Power posing
* Meditating
* Laughing
* Exercising regularly
* Listening to music
* Getting a massage
* Eliminating caffeine from our diet
* Eating a balanced, nutritious meal and eliminating processed food

Would performing any of the above activities lower our cortisol level enough to permanently change our lives? Only if the activity eliminates the dysfunctional beliefs on a subconscious level.

All of our thoughts, feelings, actions, reactions, choices, and decisions are preceded by a belief. To change our lives, the dysfunctional beliefs must be eliminated.

Power posing, listening to music, or eating a balanced meal will not permanently change our lives. Exercising will help our physical body but will not delete our dysfunctional beliefs. Laughing will bring us into the present so we will not be drawn into our fears or anger, but it will not change our lives. Meditating helps us to center and balance, but will not change our lives on a permanent basis.

To change our lives, we must be able to recognize, acknowledge, and take ownership of that which we want to change then delete the dysfunctional emotions and beliefs that preceded that what we want to change on a subconscious level.

EFT Tapping will delete dysfunctional emotions and beliefs on a subconscious level if we provide the correct "instructions" to our subconscious mind. We must word the tapping statements in the subconscious' language. We must word the tapping statement so the subconscious mind hears what we want to eliminate.

Chapter 24
Tapping Affirmations

* I am healthy and happy.
* Wealth is pouring into my life.
* I radiate love and happiness.
* I have the perfect job for me.
* I am successful in whatever I do.

If we were to tap "I am healthy and happy now" and we are not, most likely, as we are tapping, we might think, "Yeah, right. Sure. I am healthy and happy. My life sucks. I hate my job. I am always broke. There is never enough money..."

The body knows this is not true. We are not healthy and happy now. When we tap, we might have difficulty remembering what we are saying, lose focus and concentration, and/or the mind drifts.

An EFT Tapping statement is most effective **when** it matches our current belief.

The subconscious does not hear the word "No." One way of tapping affirmations and, at the same time, putting in the positives is to put the word "no" into the tapping statements.

* I am **not** healthy and happy. Subconscious hears: I am healthy and happy.
* Wealth is **not** pouring into my life. Subconscious hears: Wealth is pouring into my life.
* I **do not** radiate love and happiness. Subconscious hears: I radiate love and happiness.
* I **do not** have the perfect job for me. Subconscious hears: I have the perfect job for me.
* I am **not** successful in whatever I do. Subconscious hears: I am successful in whatever I do.

If we repeat affirmations over and over and over before we clear the affirmation with EFT Tapping, repeating the affirmation numerous times will have little effect except to create circumstances in our lives so we can be confronted with the beliefs that do not align with the affirmation.

Chapter 25
Writing Your Own EFT Tapping Statements
Rule #1 – Use Your Own Words

ELEANOR'S STORY

I am seventy-two years old. My husband of fifty years died thirteen months ago. I have been all alone since then. I do have two children and four grandchildren, but I rarely see them. We live in the same town. They are too busy to include me in their lives. I babysit and that is about it.

I am too old to start dating. I would not know how to do dating. My husband and I were high school sweethearts and got married shortly after graduating from high school. I am lonely. All my friends have either died or are dying. And, it just does not feel right to date so soon after my husband's death.

I do not know how to move beyond my grief. I do not know if I can ever be happy again. I still cry every day because I miss my husband so much. It would have been so much easier to have gone first. My husband was my best friend as well as my lover.

How do you heal a broken heart? How do I move beyond my grief? How do I start over when I am seventy-two years old? How do I stop the daily flow of tears?

Rule #1 – Using Your Own Words – EFT Tapping statements for Eleanor:

1. I am all alone.
2. I rarely see my children and grandchildren.
3. They are too busy to include me in their lives.
4. I am too old to start dating.
5. I do not know how to date.
6. I am lonely.
7. All my friends have either died or are dying.
8. It does not feel right to date so soon after my husband's death.
9. I do not know how to move beyond my grief.
10. I do not know if I can ever be happy again.

11. I cry every day because I miss my husband so much.
12. My heart is broken.
13. I do not know how to start over.

Some of the statements will desensitize the emotions; some will change the story while other statements will change the beliefs.

To heal a broken heart, we must deal with and heal grief. Eleanor might also want to heal the unwelcomed transition she has found herself in. She is lonely without her husband or other friendships. How comfortable is she with making new friends? What is her issue with making new friends?

The death of a spouse is one of the most difficult heartaches to heal. Sometimes it is so overwhelming we get stuck in the grief. When we are in overwhelm-mode we do not even know where to begin to heal.

When writing EFT Tapping statements for ourselves, we start by using our own words. We start with desensitizing painful emotions. Once our pain has lessened, then we are able to move on to other issues that need to be healed.

Matthew's Story

I am forty-six years old. The company I worked for downsized, and I am now unemployed. I have a family, a wife and three children. The kids are in their teens. The oldest just graduated from high school. I thought I would have the money to pay for his college education, and now, I cannot afford to send my son to college.

I made very good money. Since I made good money, we lived very well. Now, I have a huge mortgage. Our savings are dwindling very quickly. We are in a down economy. I am highly skilled, but these are the type of jobs that are not being filled by companies. So, what am I supposed to do?

My unemployment benefits are ending soon. I cannot afford the mortgage on my home. I cannot afford the food we eat each day. My credit cards are maxed out.

I have been searching for a job for two years. I send out resumes every day. I do not even get interviews for jobs that I am highly qualified for. I would take a lower salary if I could just find a job.

I am either over-qualified, too old, or too highly paid. When I was downsized, I thought it would be easy to find another job. I was not concerned. Now, I am. I was laid off shortly after the economy tanked.

Rule #1 – Using Your Own Words – EFT Tapping statements for Matthew:

1. I have been downsized and now I am unemployed.
2. I thought I would have the money to pay for my son's college education.
3. I cannot afford to send my son to college.
4. My savings are dwindling quickly.
5. We are in a down economy.
6. The type of job I do is not being filled by companies.
7. My unemployment benefits are ending soon.
8. I cannot afford the mortgage on my home.
9. My credit cards are maxed out.
10. I do not get interviews for jobs that I am highly qualified for.
11. I cannot find a job
12. I am over-qualified, too old, or to highly paid.
13. I am concerned that I won't find a job.

Some of the statements will desensitize the emotions, some will change the story, some will change the beliefs.

Chapter 26
Writing Your Own EFT Tapping Statements
Rule #2 – Process Emotions Before Beliefs

If we have an **emotional attachment** to a belief, it might be difficult to "let it go."

If a belief, whether constructive or destructive, healthy or dysfunctional, would put us in harm's way, we will protect ourselves. To keep us safe emotionally, we may hold onto a dysfunctional thought, feeling, and/or belief.

For example, for the beliefs that "People are cruel" and/or "The world is not a safe place," the following actions and/or reactions, thoughts and/or feelings might result:

* Fearful of new situations and the unknown.
* Fearful of being rejected and/or abandoned because we feel we are damaged goods.
* Feel as if everything is hopeless.
* Feel ashamed when we are ridiculed for being inadequate.
* Fears that could undermine and destroy relationships.
* Fear of conflict, criticism, and being judged.
* Being terrified of everything.
* Believing that sorrow is our lot in life.
* Constantly feeling inferior and less than others.
* Getting lost in our self-pity and shame.
* Taking and making most things personal.
* Feel undesirable and unwanted.
* Feeling anxious about everything.
* Feel helpless and powerless.

These emotions can be processed and tapped. EFT Tapping statements must be personal about ourselves. Thus, the statements are in the first person, "Me" or "I." Turn the feelings into a tapping statement. We can only heal that which we recognize and acknowledge in ourselves.

* I am afraid of new situations and the unknown.
* I am damaged goods.
* I fear rejection, abandonment, and heartache.
* I feel everything is hopeless.
* I am riddled with shame.
* I feel inadequate.
* I fear conflict, criticism, and being judged.
* Sorrow is my lot in life.

* I constantly feel inferior and less than others.
* My fears undermine and destroy my relationships.
* I am lost in self-pity and shame.
* I take and make most things personal.
* I feel undesirable and unwanted.
* I am anxious about everything.
* I feel helpless and powerless.

All these feelings are the result of the belief that people are cruel and the world is an unsafe place.

> If we have an emotional attachment to a belief, it might be difficult to "let it go."
>
> If a belief, whether constructive or destructive, healthy or dysfunctional, would put us in harm's way, we will protect ourselves. To keep us safe emotionally, we may hold onto a dysfunctional thought, feeling, and/or belief.

Some like to finish their tapping with statements that are centering and calming. If this is you, then you might want to try the sixteen statements on the next page or make up those that you like. The statements can be said in any order that works for you.

Tapping Location	Statement
Eyebrow	All is well in my life.
Temple	Every day in every way I am getting better and better.
Under the Eye	I am fulfilled in every way, every day.
Under the Nose	My blessings appears in rich appropriate form with divine timing.
Under the Lips	I am an excellent steward of wealth and
Under the Collarbone Knob	I take complete responsibility for everything in my life.
Under the Arm	I have all the tools, skills, and abilities to excel in my life.
Top back part of the Head	I know I will be able to handle anything that arises in my life.
Eyebrow	All my dreams, hopes, wishes, and goals are being fulfilled each and every day.
Temple	Divine love expressing through me, now draws to me new ideas.
Under the Eye	I am comfortable with my life changing.
Under the Nose	I am able to create all that I desire.
Under the Lips	I know what needs to be done and follow through to completion.
Under the Collarbone Knob	My health is perfect in every way, physically, mentally, emotionally, and spiritually.
Under the Arm	I invite into my subconscious Archangel Raphael to heal all that needs to be forgiven, released, and redeemed. Cleanse me and free me from it now.
Top back part of the Head	The light of God surrounds me. The love of God enfolds me. The power of God protects me. The presence of God watches over and flows through me.

Chapter 28
Summary

* An EFT Tapping statement has three parts:
    1. "Even though"
    2. Instructions to the subconscious,
    3. Ending with "I totally and completely accept myself."

* Everything in our life is a direct result of our beliefs.

* A belief is a mental acceptance of the actuality of something whether it is Truth or not.

* A dysfunctional belief takes us away from peace, joy, and love.

* Beliefs precede all thoughts, feelings, decisions, choices, actions, reactions, and experiences.

* The conscious mind is the part of us that thinks, passes judgments, makes decisions, remembers, analyzes, has desires, and communicates with others. It is responsible for logic and reasoning, understanding and comprehension.

* The subconscious mind is the storehouse of our beliefs. It does not evaluate, make decisions, or pass judgment; it just is. It does not determine if something is "right" or "wrong."

* If we want to make changes in our lives, long-lasting, permanent, constructive changes, we must change the destructive, dysfunctional beliefs in the subconscious mind. We have to change the programming in the subconscious.

* Three rules of the subconscious: Personal, Positive, Present time.

* As blocked energy can flow more freely because of EFT Tapping, the body is able to "breathe a sigh of relief." Yawning is an indication that energy is able to flow more freely along the meridians.

* After tapping, we need some downtime for integration to take place when the physical body and the mind are "idle."

* Acceptance brings us into present time. We can only heal if we are in present time.

* EFT addresses the current dysfunctional beliefs on a subconscious level.

* Tapping allows our Truth to come forth.

* Tapping allows our own body's Infinite Wisdom to move us toward healing.

* By changing the dysfunctional emotions and beliefs on a subconscious level, the changes we make with EFT are **permanent.**

* Tapping neutralizes stored memories.

* Tapping desensitizes us to hurtful and painful situations.

* What we say as we tap is very important. The tapping statements we make as we tap are the instructions for the subconscious mind.

* EFT Tapping statements are most effective when they agree with the current belief. The body is less likely to sabotage a tapping statement and the process if the tapping statement agrees with the current belief.

* When we use "no" in an EFT Tapping statement, the subconscious doesn't hear the "no." We only care what the subconscious hears. When we say, "I am not going to eat that piece of cake," the subconscious hears, "Yum, cake!"

* Our inner critic and negative self-talk are our teachers. They are letting us know the path to healing, to well-being, and to peace.

* One statement per round of EFT Tapping is beneficial for eliminating dysfunctional beliefs.

* Multiple statements per round are beneficial to desensitize painful emotions and/or story.

* Tapping both sides is not as beneficial as tapping only one side. Tapping one side acts more like a pattern interrupt for our Infinite Wisdom to surface.

* There is no difference between tapping the long form of EFT vs the short form.

* EFT Tapping can be used anytime, anyplace, for anything.

* EFT Tapping can be used for anything we don't want anymore.

* The very first tapping statement needs to be: "It's not okay or safe for my life to change."

* Walking forward represents forward movement in our lives. Walking backward represents the past. Physical movement can help clear emotional issues and facilitate change. Walking backward undoes the past and helps clear, heal, and transform an issue in our lives.

* One measure of knowing how much an "issue" has been "resolved" is to begin, before tapping, by giving the issue an intensity number between 1 – 10, with 10 being high. Giving an issue an intensity level indicates the progress we are making with resolving and/or healing that issue as tap.

* Lowering cortisol levels is not enough to permanently change our lives.

* Tapping a statement that may not have cleared over and over and over again will not clear the statement. What beliefs might be underneath the statement that will not clear? Tap the underlying beliefs.

* If a tapping statement does not clear, turn the statement into a question. Tap the answer(s).

* If an issue we tapped persists, we didn't process the correct issue. Turn the issue around and look at it from a different perspective.

* Three possible reasons that EFT Tapping may not have worked:
  1) The tapping statement might not be worded such that a dysfunctional belief and/or emotion is addressed and eliminated.
  2) The style of tapping, laser-focused vs. round robin, may not be appropriate for the issue to be resolved or statements to clear.
  3) Tapping on a symptom and not addressing the cause of the issue, thus the tapping may not have been as effective.

* Repeating affirmations might not be beneficial until the affirmation is tapped by adding a "no" into the tapping statement.

* Rule #1 for Writing Your Own EFT Tapping Statements is to use your own words.

* Rule #2 for Writing Your Own EFT Tapping Statements is to process emotions before beliefs.

EFT Tapping Stories

1) Pete's Story for Healing the Self
2) Katherine, Megan, and Beau's Story for
Dealing with Obnoxious People

Chapter 29
Pete's Story

After striking out, Pete walks back to the bench in a daze. Normally, Pete is the heavy-duty slugger when at bat. If there are runners on base, Pete usually ensures that the runners score. Not today though. Third time to bat and Pete has struck out again.

"Slugger," says Charlie cheerfully, as he sits down next to Pete. "Where are you? Certainly not in the game. I know this isn't the big leagues. It isn't even the little leagues. Hey, it's only for fun. It doesn't seem as if you are having any fun though."

"Huh?" Pete, sitting up, looks at Charlie. "Charlie, how long have you known me?"

Laughing, Charlie responds, "Seems like forever, but to answer your question, since the 6th grade, when we were in Little League together."

Seriously, Pete asks, "Did I always want to be a businessman?"

"Hardly," Charlie answers.

"When did I want to go into business? I don't remember," Pete says.

Confused, Charlie asks, "Seriously, you don't remember at the beginning of your senior year when your mom started talking to you about colleges?"

Struggling to remember, Pete says, "Vaguely."

"Seriously?" asks a stunned Charlie. Looking over at Pete, he can tell that Pete doesn't remember, so he adds, "Your mom started talking to you about colleges at the beginning of our senior year. She wanted you to go to a college that had a good business department. She thought you should major in business."

A little surprised, Pete looks back at Charlie and says, "I thought we were looking at colleges that had a good baseball team and scholarships."

With humor, Charlie says, "You were looking at the baseball team of the colleges that your mom thought you should attend."

Puzzled, Pete looks back at the field, trying to remember.

After sitting quietly for a few minutes and realizing that Pete is back in never-never land, Charlie, with compassion in his voice, asks, "So, Slugger, what's going on? Want to clue me in?" Still looking at the field, Pete dryly says, "I was offered a promotion at work."

Happy for his friend, Charlie says with excitement, "Wow! Congratulations!" When Pete continues to look at the field, Charlie takes this as a clue that Pete isn't as excited about this promotion. "So, this is not good news?"

Sitting up tall, Pete looks back at Charlie and says without emotion, "I don't know. I'm not excited about it." Looking back at the baseball field, Pete rests his arms on his legs.

"I can see that," says Charlie. "What's the rest of the story?"

"I don't know, Charlie. I don't know." Slowly, Pete sits up straight as if uncoiling, looks over at Charlie, and says, "I have worked hard for this promotion. It's been my focus for so long, and now that it's here, I have no passion or excitement for the promotion, for work, or for business. I am beginning to realize work and business don't excite me anymore, and I wonder if they ever did."

Charlie isn't sure what to ask Pete about: his lack of passion for business, or what would make him happy. This is news to him that Pete isn't passionate about business.

Pete asks, "Charlie, what am I doing with my life?"

"Pete," Charlie starts, "When did you realize that you weren't passionate about business?"

Thinking for a bit, Pete finally responds, "I don't think I was ever passionate about business."

Charlie asks Pete, "Wouldn't you have known in college if you weren't passionate about business? I mean, you declared business as your major from the get-go."

"In college, Charlie, the only thing that I cared about was baseball. I don't think either of us ever missed a practice or game," Pete says.

Laughing, Charlie adds, "I knew if I missed a practice, you would yell louder at me than coach! So, I didn't dare miss a practice."

Taking a deep breath, Pete says, "Every time I run onto the field, Charlie, I feel happy. I feel free. I don't think about work—or anything, actually. Just baseball."

"It sounds like you are searching for some answers. I have a solution. Remember the EFT tapping that I do?" Charlie asks.

"I do know you do that tapping thing. I don't know what it is or how to do it," Pete says.

"Yup, that tapping thing. My mentor is teaching a class this afternoon, and Melinda and I are help with the logistics. Come with us this afternoon. I promise you will find some of the answers that you are searching for. Scout's honor," Charlie says.

"Charlie!" exclaims Pete. "You were never a Scout, Boy Scout, Cub Scout, or any other kind of Scout for that matter! Not much of a guarantee!"

"Okay, Pete. You want a guarantee?" Charlie pauses, thinking, then says, "I will give you one. A guarantee, that is. If the class or EFT tapping are not helpful at all, I will do your chores around the house for a week!"

"Ah," says Pete. "Making an offer I can't refuse. You know that I hate doing chores. Next week is my turn to mow the lawn. If I'm not convinced there is something to this tapping thing, you will mow the lawn, right?"

"I must be serious because you know how much I hate mowing the lawn, too." Charlie adds, "Hey, Pete, since both of us hate mowing the lawn, and we are both employed and rich at this time, let's hire someone to mow our lawn."

"Great idea," Pete says cheerfully. "Since you thought of the idea, you have the responsibility of hiring someone. Oh, and this does not let you out of our bet. You still have to mow the lawn next week if I don't think the class is helpful."

"That's cool. You still have to mow the lawn next week if the class is helpful. And I already know who we're going to hire. Johnny, the kid next door, asked last week if he could mow our lawn. Told him that I would talk to you. I just did, so Johnny can start the week after next," Charlie says. Then, with a huge smile on his face, he adds, "I know it won't be me cutting the grass next week."

After the game ends, Charlie and Pete head home to shower before going to Grace's class on EFT tapping. On the way, Charlie and Pete stop to pick up Melinda, Charlie's girlfriend. The three of them are the first to arrive. After Charlie introduces Pete to Grace, Grace says with a genuine smile on her face, "Ah, the infamous Pete, Charlie's best friend and partner in crime. That Pete?"

Turning a little red, Pete says, "I'm not sure that's the best way to start a class. Anything that I can do to make a better impression?"

"Actually, there is, Pete," says Grace. "Can you help Charlie put up the signs and flags that help people find us? That would go a long way in making a great impression."

"Happy to help," responds Pete with a smile, before turning to find Charlie.

After helping Charlie, as people begin arriving for class, Pete wanders around the classroom, viewing all the informative posters on the wall.

When class is about to start, Charlie finds a seat near the front, off to the right side. Grace begins the class, informing the students that it is a basic class on EFT tapping. She says that she likes to jump right in and have the students experience EFT tapping before she explains what EFT tapping is. After asking for a volunteer, a brave soul quickly gets to her feet and scurries to the front.

After asking the student her name, Grace says to the student, Pricilla, "I'm going to ask you a question. Your immediate response will be, 'Sure it is.' Before you respond, I ask that you think about the question before giving me the immediate response." Pricilla nods her head in understanding.

The question that Grace asks Pricilla is if it is okay and safe for her life to change. Pricilla ponders the question and finally says, "My immediate response would have been, 'Oh, sure it's okay and safe for my life to change.' Yet, thinking about the question, I realize that it's more complex than you would think. Our lives are constantly changing, but that doesn't mean we are comfortable with change, or that it is safe to change. I would have to answer the question 'No.' On my honeymoon, I didn't speak to my husband on the first day. I couldn't get used to the idea that I would be a Mrs. for the rest of my life."

Grace asks Pricilla, "Are you still married?"

Smiling, Pricilla holds up her left hand and shows Grace the wedding ring. "I was fortunate to marry a man who was and is very forgiving. Actually, we just became empty-nesters, and our lives are going through huge changes right now."

"I would like to make it okay and safe for your life to change, particularly now that you and your husband have to adapt to a new life and way of being," says Grace.

"That would be such a blessing and a relief. I don't want to be the clingy mom, unable to let go of her children, and I don't want to do something that my husband would have to forgive me for," says Pricilla with an expression of gratitude.

When Grace asks Pricilla if she is familiar with a technique called muscle testing, Pricilla responds in the affirmative. Grace turns to the class and explains the specifics of muscle testing to those who do not have a clue what it is. She explains that muscle testing is a way to bypass the conscious mind and ask the body questions. Charlie and Melinda have muscle tested each other before at home, so Pete has some familiarity with it, but that is the extent of what he knows.

When Grace asks Pricilla's body if it is okay and safe for her life to change, the body answers with a "negative" response. Pricilla says, "No surprise."

"In 30 seconds, we can delete that dysfunctional belief," says Grace.

With enthusiasm, Pricilla responds with, "Lead on, Grace, I'm ready to change now and have it be okay and safe for my life to change!" The class chuckles at Pricilla's animated response.

"Okay, Pricilla, I lead, you echo," says Grace.

After one round of EFT tapping, Grace asks Pricilla's body if it is okay and safe for her life to change. When the body's response is in the "affirmative," Pricilla begins her happy dance. In case the class didn't know that it was her happy dance, she tells everyone! Laughing at Pricilla, Grace thanks her for being an exceptional volunteer. Pricilla continues her happy dance as she makes her way back to her seat.

Pete doesn't know what to think. He doesn't know if the muscle testing is for real. He doesn't know if a belief can be changed in 30 seconds just by tapping his head. He sits in his seat a little dazed.

Then Grace begins the explanation of EFT tapping. "We asked Pricilla's body if it was okay and safe for her life to change. Her body said, 'No.' The physical body is here to protect us. If our hand gets too close to a flame, our body will automatically pull the hand back to safety."

Moving to the front of the classroom, Grace continues. "We made a statement as we tapped. We said, 'Even though it's not okay or safe for my life to change, I totally and completely accept myself.' This statement appeases the physical body.

"At the end of the statement, we said, 'I totally and completely accept myself.' Acceptance brings us into present time." Walking to the whiteboard, Grace continues, "We can only heal if we are in present time. Fear is about the future. Anger is about the present. Healing takes place in the present."

Grace writes on the whiteboard: "Agree with the current belief" and "Healing occurs only in the present."

Walking back to the front of the classroom, Grace continues, "If we want to make changes in our lives, we must change the programming. Just as a computer can only do what it has been programmed to do, we can only do what we have been programmed to do. Our beliefs determine our programming. The beliefs are stored in the subconscious mind." Grace walks back to the whiteboard and writes: "We can only do what we have been programmed to do. Our beliefs determine our programming. Beliefs are stored in the subconscious mind."

Facing the class again, Grace says, "If we want to make changes in our lives, we must change the dysfunctional beliefs on a subconscious level. It's the only way we change. We must remove, delete, eliminate the dysfunctional beliefs on the subconscious level."

Turning back to the whiteboard, she writes: "Beliefs precede all of our thoughts and feelings, choices and decisions, and actions and reactions." As she turns to face the class, she says, "All of our thoughts and feelings, actions and reactions, and choices and decisions are a result of our beliefs. Change a belief to change a life."

Grace now writes on the whiteboard: "Personal. Present time. Positive."

Facing the class, Grace continues, "The subconscious has three rules that I like. They all start with 'P.' Personal, Present time, and Positive. The subconscious only knows the self. The first 'P' is for Personal."

Walking back to the front of the room, she says, "Present time—the subconscious only understands 'Now.' When you say, 'I am going to start my diet tomorrow,' tomorrow never comes, and thus, we never start the diet. We must be specific and say, 'February 1st, 2016, I will start my diet.' When February 1st rolls around, the body says, 'Time to start the diet.' Subconscious only understands present time."

Making eye contact with her students, Grace adds, "And, the last 'P' is for Positive, the most important rule of the subconscious. The subconscious only understands the positive. How many of you have children?" About half the class raises their hands. When you tell your child 'Don't slam the door,' what do they do?" Everyone in class knew the answer: They slam the door!

"Yup, you're right. They slam the door. You gave them a command: 'Don't slam the door.' Subconscious does not hear the word 'No.' You gave them the command: 'Slam the door.' Most times, if not all the time, they slam the door," Grace says, as a few heads start to nod up and down in a new awareness.

Grace continues, "How many of you have said, 'I am not going to eat that piece of cake,' and end up eating the cake. You gave yourself a command: 'Eat that piece of cake.' You end up eating the cake." This time, Grace notices a few jaws drop open in a new awareness.

"The solution?" asks Grace. "Tell yourself and other people what you want, not what you don't want." Grace moves back to the whiteboard and writes: "Tell people what you want and not what you don't want."

Even though Pete is not one to speak up in class or ask questions, he is dumbfounded. He raises his hand. When Grace calls on Pete, he asks, "What's the tapping significance?"

"Great lead into the next part of the explanation on how EFT tapping works," says Grace. "We know from Traditional Oriental medicine that there are energy pathways in the body called meridians. When we tap, we are tapping on points along the various energy meridians in the body. The tapping is like a pattern interrupt for our own body's Infinite Wisdom to come forth."

Again, Pete puts up his hand and asks, "What does a body's Infinite Wisdom mean?"

A smiling Grace says, "Our body has an Infinite Wisdom. If we cut our finger, our body knows what to do to heal the cut. We don't have to tell the body to stop bleeding and mend the skin. When the body and the environment are healthy, the body automatically will gravitate to health, wealth, and well-being. After the cut is healed, we usually don't even remember cutting our finger."

Pete asks another question, "How does this relate to EFT tapping?"

In response, Grace says, "When we tap, we are healing the dysfunctional beliefs and emotions. Once the dysfunctional beliefs have been eliminated, our bodies will automatically gravitate to health, wealth, and well-being."

Meeting the eyes of the student, Grace continues, "With tapping, integration needs to take place for the changes to take effect. Just as a computer must be rebooted when the programming has changed, we require the same thing. Usually, for us, this means sleep or downtime in which the body is idle or doing nothing. Most times when we tap, we wake up the next day and don't remember what we processed or the pain that we were in before we tapped. Integration has happened. For some of my clients, it might take up to three or four days to integrate."

Stopping to think, Grace decides and says, "I would like Pete and two other students to come up to the front."

Feeling as if he is in trouble, Pete reluctantly moves to the front of the classroom, as well as another male and female students. "We're going to tap now. Before we do, I want to see if it is okay and safe for these three students' lives to change." Grace muscle tests each of the three students. It is not okay or safe for the lives of any of the three to change.

"Class, I want you to follow along and do as I do. I want you to echo the statements that I make," Grace instructs. At the end, Grace says, "Take a deep breath and exhale. Good. Let's see how our volunteers did."

Pete does not feel like a volunteer. Regardless, he is glad that he is one of them. He wants to experience the muscle testing for himself.

"Remember," says Grace, "it only took one finger when I muscle tested before, when the answer was 'no.' When I muscle test this time, watch my bicep and see how much energy I am exerting on their arms."

Grace starts with Pete. When Grace exerts pressure on his arm, Pete's arm stays strong and rigid. Pete's surprise is evident on his face. "You seem surprised, Pete," says a smiling Grace.

"Truthfully, I am surprised. It's beyond my ability to understand. This seems too good to be true," says a confused Pete.

Laughing, Grace says, "It was mine, as well. Sixteen years ago, I went searching for a tool to help my clients fulfill the tasks that they said they would perform that week but never completed. A friend recommended a book on EFT tapping. As I was reading the book, I thought it was stupid. How could tapping my head change my life? At the time, I had some trusting and forgiving clients whom I taught how to tap. When each one of them told me the remarkable difference in their lives that week, I took notice. And now, tapping is my go-to, favorite tool to help my clients."

Turning to the class, she adds, "EFT might seem like a simple, uncomplicated process, yet this simple tool is quite effective for changing our lives."

Moving down the line, Grace muscle tests the other two volunteers who also prove to be strong after tapping "It's not okay and safe for my life to change."

"Charlie and Melinda are passing out the handout for the class, as well as a blank note card," says Grace. "We're going to take a short break here. If there is anything that you want to heal, resolve, or understand, write it down on the note cards and hand them to Melinda and Charlie. I want the class to be relevant to the issues that you have in your lives right now."

Pete looks around the class and watches the majority of students fill up both sides of their note cards. A few people even ask for additional note cards. Pete is conflicted on whether he should be writing his questions out, as well.

"You look perplexed, Pete," says Charlie.

"Oh, hi. I didn't hear you come up," answers Pete.

Chuckling, Charlie says, "You looked deep in thought. Trying to decide if you should ask a question or two?"

"Actually, I was," responds Pete.

"After class, Grace usually takes Melinda and me out to dinner to thank us for volunteering. Would you like to join us?" asks Charlie.

"Oh, I wouldn't want to intrude. But since you are asking, I accept as long as I can pay for my own dinner," says Pete.

"I don't think I will be mowing the lawn next week," teases Charlie.

"Class has not concluded yet!" Pete reminds Charlie.

The remainder of the class is spent reading each and every note card, helping the students find their own answers, and then learning how to use EFT tapping to heal the issue. With each note card that Grace reads, the more impressed Pete becomes.

At dinner, Pete makes a decision. He wants Grace to help him find his answers and solutions for his life. Grace says that she would love to help Pete discover his truths.

*****

Pete had a session with Grace once a week. He found it helpful to talk to Charlie after a session. Charlie and Pete had known each other and been each other's best friend for a long time. Not only were they roommates now but they were also roommates all four years in college.

Pete found the exploration of himself fascinating, fulfilling, and exciting. Grace pushed him to think creatively in terms of himself. He enjoyed the tapping that they did together in the sessions, as well as the tapping homework that he tapped in between sessions.

Pete came to realize that he was living his mother's version of what she wanted for his life. When Grace asked Pete what brought him joy and made him happy, it took him a month of digging to remember that he enjoyed his involvement with children. He had dated a woman in college who was majoring in child development. He sometimes tagged along when she had an assignment off-campus, working with children. He thought that he was tagging along to make sure she was safe. Now, he realized that he enjoyed the involvement and interactivity with the kids. He loved teaching them how to catch a ball or swing a bat.

How could he have forgotten the joy that he found in the faces of the kids whom he taught how to dribble a ball down a court or swing a tennis racket?

After a month of working with Grace and beginning his self-exploration, Pete decided that he wanted to do something with kids. He was a little intimidated by the prospect of doing something that he wasn't trained to do. Charlie was a Little League coach. Pete thought maybe that would be a good place to start. Pete asked Charlie if he would mentor him and shadow Charlie to learn how to work with children. Charlie's response was, "Bro, you just can't get enough of me. I love it! You can be the equipment manager in charge of hauling all the bats and balls around."

Pete, knowing his boss would find his self-exploration frivolous and excessive, did not mention any of this to him. He did need to leave earlier in the day to be able to make the Little League practices. Pete told his boss that he wanted to coach a Little League team. A parent himself of two little boys who played Little League, Pete thought his boss might be understanding. Or he could be a jerk and say no. Pete wasn't sure how he would respond. He asked his boss if he could come in early, so he could leave earlier to make practice. His boss was fine with the new arrangement, as long as his work didn't suffer and make him regret giving him the promotion.

Realizing that he was living his mother's life that she wanted for him, Pete talked with his parents. His mom told him that she always thought Pete would be a professional ball player and business could have been a good backup option. As a parent, she knew his love and involvement with baseball created a singular focus for him and was concerned for him when baseball was no longer an option. The only thing that she wanted for him was to be happy and fulfilled. If that meant leaving the business world, he was an adult able to make his own decisions of what was best for him, what would bring him joy. She had always supported her son and would continue to support him in whatever he decided to do. She did add that one day she would love to be a grandmother, which wasn't news to Pete.

When Grace asked Pete the ten adjectives or attributes that he wanted to describe himself, he was stumped. Grace told Pete that when the subconscious knows the manner in which Pete wants to describe himself, the subconscious goes to work to make it so.

Pete had no clue which attributes he wanted to define and pattern his life. Knowing that Charlie had most likely already completed this task in one of Grace's classes, he asked Charlie which attributes he might consider for himself. Charlie was his normal Charlie-self and rattled off so many that Pete's head started to swim...compassion, warmth, understanding, powerful, wise, allowing, confident, perceptive, grounded, congruent, imaginative, courageous, accepting, charismatic, nurturing, content, determined, persistent, focused, gracious, happy, insightful, receptive, intelligent, motivated, optimistic, passionate, curious, problem-solver, reliable, respectful. Pete pulled out a pad and started writing as Charlie erupted with ideas.

Session after session, Grace challenged Pete to think creatively about himself and his life. Using EFT tapping and fulfilling the assignments that Grace assigned, slowly Pete began to understand who he was, what made him happy, and how to use EFT tapping to heal the parts of himself that were no longer of value.

Pete enjoyed the process of self-discovery with a knowledgeable guide along the way. Grace made the process fun and exciting. Each session was another adventure into the life of Pete O'Toole.

Having a friend like Charlie Baker, who had known him for eons, was a blessing. Charlie tells it like it is. When you give him permission, he doesn't hold back. He will tell the whole truth from his perspective, which is usually right on target.

It has now been a year since Pete began this process of self-discovery. Pete has gone back to college, taking classes on how to be a coach. Since his work did not suffer when he started leaving early for Little League practice, Pete's boss is allowing him to adjust his work schedule to accommodate his class schedule.

Pete has decided that he wants to augment this business career by coaching children or teenagers. His college classes and helping Charlie with his Little Leaguers are giving him the tools, skills, and confidence that he needs to be able to work with younger generations.

Chapter 30
Katherine, Megan, and Beau's Story

As the family car pulls up in front of the house, Megan and Beau run out to meet their big sister, Katherine.

"It's been three long years since I have had all my children home for Thanksgiving," says Mom excitedly as she steps out of the car.

Dad adds as he exits the driver's seat, "You three have made your mom a very happy lady today. Beau, help me with your sister's luggage."

Megan opens the door and Katherine steps out into the late afternoon sunshine. "Nice to feel the sunshine on your face after leaving a dreary day in the Northwest?" Megan asks as she hugs her sister.

"And don't forget the busy, crazy, crowded airport and airplane!" says Katherine. "It is soooo good to be home and to see everyone." Looking back at her parents, she adds, "Thanks, Mom and Dad, for picking me up at the airport."

As Beau helps Dad retrieve Katherine's luggage from the trunk of the car, he shouts out playfully to Katherine, "Think you brought enough? Good thing I'm a strong guy or else you would have to carry your own luggage into the house!"

"Ha, ha. I see college hasn't changed that sharp, quick wit of yours," says a smiling Katherine. "Give me a hug, here and now, young man," demands Katherine. Beau drops her bag and obeys his sister.

As the five enter the house, before running off to the kitchen, Mom remarks, "It's been three years since we celebrated Thanksgiving together. Katherine, I am so glad that you could get away. To celebrate, I'm cooking some of everyone's favorite foods. Sit down here in the living room and chat while your dad while I finish preparing dinner." With that, the three siblings sink into their favorite chairs.

"Wow, the last time I was home was for your graduation, Beau," Katherine says. "I can't believe it's been so long. Time flies."

"Yup, you were just starting your new job with the dot com start-up company. Megan just turned pro. And, that summer, I moved to live on campus. Fortunately, I live close enough that I can still come home and allow Mom to wash my clothes!" says a smiling Beau.

Teasingly, Megan says, "Once the baby, always the baby. Mom's favorite."

"Hey, can I help it if I'm smart, good looking, and a sweet son?"

"Ha. Ha," chuckles Megan. "Don't forget athletic, successful, and popular, along with that description of yourself."

"I was being modest," declares Beau.

Reflecting, Megan says, "Oh, yes. I forgot 'modest' and maybe I should also add 'thoughtful,' 'endearing,' 'brave' and 'kind.'"

All three of the siblings laugh. Katherine interjects, "I see not much has changed between the two of you. Nice to be home even if the two of you still tease each other."

"The track club is only three hours away, so I'm able to come home often to see Mom and Dad and they do come to my local meets," notes Megan.

"Even though," Katherine starts, "I'm hundreds of miles away, Mom keeps me updated on your success. After each meet, she emails me a recap of your performance."

Megan sits on her cushion and beams ear to ear. "It is nice having Mom and Dad at the meets. I can definitely hear them when they cheer me on. I'm injury-free this year and only being twenty-five, I think I have my best years still ahead of me."

"Your turn, Katherine," states Beau. "Catch us up with what's going on with the dot com company."

Seeing and hearing a heavy sigh from Katherine, Beau becomes alarmed. "Everything okay? Are you still working with the dot com company? Or did they not make it? It's a tough economy to start a new business." Asking again, Beau says, "Everything okay, Sis?"

"Well," says Katherine after another heavy sigh, "the dot com company is still in start-up. We're only three years old. Lots of growing pains." She pauses.

"Come on Sis. Fess up," demands Megan. "What gives? Is this part of the reason you came home? You haven't been home since you started the new job. You don't like your job? Don't like the Northwest? Don't like your boss? What's going on?"

"Being your big sister, I feel like I'm supposed to be an example for the two of you. I'm supposed to have it all together. After all I am twenty-eight years old," Katherine says, trying to act sophisticated.

Softening her tone, Megan asks, "By whose rules are you supposed to have it all together? No one in this house or family. So, it sounds like you are home to figure something out. Want to share?"

"Megan, you always did have a beat on your siblings," Katherine says, trying to smile.

Both Beau and Megan sit quietly while Katherine gathers her thoughts. She looks at one, then the other. "I don't want either of you to think I'm a coward or running away or a wimp." She pauses, looking out the window, Katherine gathers her thoughts.

Knowing that Beau was about to make a comment, Megan shoots him one of her "Don't you dare say anything sarcastic" looks. Beau closes his mouth and waits for Katherine to start up again.

Turning back her head to look at her siblings, Katherine begins, "I was hired because I had a degree in social media, communication, and journalism. Bob was hired because he was the owner's nephew."

With curiosity, Beau asks, "I don't remember Bob's resume and credentials. What's his degree in?"

"Well, Bob doesn't have a degree. Bob never went to college," answers Katherine.

Figuring it out, Megan says, "So, Bob's only credential is that he is the boss' nephew."

"You were always the smart one, Megan," Katherine says.

Beau, not to be outdone by his sister says, "He knows nothing. You are supposed to train him. And, he takes advantage of the fact that he is the boss' nephew."

"I do have two insightful and intuitive siblings!" exclaims Katherine. "Both of you are correct."

Megan replies, "Well, it's not hard to figure out. It's rare that you are unhappy. It didn't sound like the boss or the location were the issues. Knowing you, we speculated."

With compassion, Beau says, "So, tell us what's going on."

"I think my biggest complaint," Katherine starts, "is that he takes credit for everything I do. After trying to deal with him for three years, now he ends up bringing out the worst in me. He exploits and devalues me, sometimes in front of our boss! His teasing and flirting is irritating. As if I would even think of him in a romantic way!"

Megan inquires, "What did your boss say when you talked to him about Bob?"

Katherine responds, "I haven't talked to him about Bob."

A little amazed, Beau asks, "Why not?"

Katherine answers, "What am I supposed to say? 'Bob takes credit for all my successes'? 'When anything goes wrong, he blames me instead of taking any responsibility'? 'He sucks my energy dry?' 'I'm ill-equipped to deal with Bob'? 'He makes me feel angry and frustrated'? And how do you think my boss would respond?"

Beau answers, "We don't know. We don't know how he would respond. And neither do you. You haven't talked to him."

"Bob is a totally different person when his uncle is around," says Katherine. "And I'm supposed to point out to my boss that his nephew is an irresponsible, stupid, blameless jerk?"

Megan thinks for a minute then says, "What are your options? Bob is a jerk. You have not said anything to your boss. Instead, you are trying to figure out if you want to quit because of Bob. Have you at least thought of talking to your boss?"

"No," says Katherine as she shakes her head side to side.

Megan says, "And your reasoning is that it's his nephew and like the nephew, he would not value you, take you seriously, and think the problem is you and not Bob. Blood is thicker than water?"

"Something like that," Katherine says confidently.

Beau reminds Katherine, "That's not the way we were raised, Katherine."

Unconvinced Katherine says, "It's one thing to be outspoken in your own home, where it is safe to do so. It's not safe for me to speak ill of the boss' nephew to the boss."

Beau reassures her, "You won't know until you talk to your boss. He just might surprise you."

"I should not have to change me because of him," says Katherine feeling exhaustion. "I am so tired of being talked to. So tired of his 'only kidding' remarks. So tired of his humorless jokes."

Beau probes a little deeper. "And the reason you have not spoken to your boss?"

"Cause Bob is right outside the door!" exclaims Katherine. "I think it would be so much easier on the track! You can do your own thing without having a boss to deal with. True, you have a coach, but a coach is someone on your team, helping you to be all that you can be and do!"

Both Megan and Beau laugh! Little did she know!

"Katherine, there is not a neon sign on the track that says, 'Jerks, stay away.' I'm dealing with an obnoxious person as well."

"Seriously?" says an amazed Katherine.

"Oh, you might have to deal with a jerk, but I have a narcissist, a flamboyant narcissist that has singled me out to irritate. Grrr," says Megan.

Katherine asks, "How so?"

With emphasis, Megan announces, "She is pompous and condescending. She feels she is superior to everyone. She is brash, loud, and obnoxious. Julie thinks the entire world revolves around her. No one and nothing exists other than her needs!"

"That's putting it mildly," adds Beau. "I've met Julie. She makes no bones that she is the best, even though she is not. She is self-centered, self-absorbed, a braggart, and a show-off."

"Whoa! And she can get away with this with all the other athletes on the team?" asks Katherine.

"She just doesn't care what anyone else says or thinks," remarks Megan. "I think what hurts the most is she befriended me when I joined the team. After being stabbed in the back and betrayed, I realized that a friendship with me was all an act. She saw me as the competition and wanted to destroy my self-confidence. Her intent was to hurt me! Mission accomplished! I felt very betrayed and hurt and she thinks it funny that I feel that way. Beau happened to be home the weekend I ended up here in tears."

"Not a pretty sight," adds Beau. "Lots of tears, hurt feelings, and feelings of betrayal. You don't want to meet this woman."

With empathy, Katherine asks if Megan had talked to the coach.

Shrugging her shoulder, Megan replies, "I don't see any point. The coach doesn't do anything. Julie gets away with stuff that he doesn't allow anyone else to get away with. He treats her like a prima donna, which just feeds into her 'I'm better than anyone else's attitude.'"

"Whoa, guess I'm not the only one dealing with an obnoxious person," Katherine proclaims.

Shaking her head from side to side, Megan laughingly says, "How right you are. Beau, tell Katherine about the teaching assistant you are dealing with." Megan couldn't help herself. She had to laugh. Katherine looks at Megan, questioning her reaction!

With a deep sigh, Beau begins his saga, "Oh, the TA. In one of my classes, the professor has a TA that grades the exams and papers. On the multiple choice questions, I get one of the highest scores on the exam. When it comes to the essay questions and papers, I get Cs and Ds."

Looking dismayed and confused, "Cs? And Ds? You?" Katherine couldn't believe what she was hearing. "You've always been on the Dean's List and maintain a higher grade point average than any of your fellow students. What's going on?"

"Talk about pompous and condescending," Beau laughs. "Yup. This TA is very critical and judgmental of me. He's jealous of who he perceives me to be. He told me that my good looks and athletic abilities would not ensure me a good grade."

"What is he talking about? You have always worked hard for your grades," Katherine says with disbelief. "True, you have Dad's good looks and athletic abilities, but you would never expect your success to be a result of either. When you aren't on the field, you always have your nose in a book."

Smiling, Beau shrugs. "He won't listen to reason." He begins to pace back and forth in the living room. "When I try to talk to him, he thinks I am badgering him and trying to intimidate him." Returning to his seat, he adds, "He is kind of wimpy. He's not happy and certainly not fulfilled. He sees I have a girlfriend, do well in baseball, my grades are always the highest, which he thinks the other professors grace me with because I play sports and that I have not earned my high marks."

Scowling, Katherine says, "He sounds mean and vengeful, and jealous of you."

"I agree. Trying to talk to him is like pulling teeth. Painful," adds Beau.

Katherine inquires, "What does the professor say?"

Megan answers, "I think he should talk to the professor. Beau doesn't want to."

"I don't want to seem like a wimp or asking for special consideration," Beau mentions.

Megan responds, "Are you going to allow one insecure TA to ruin your GPA? What's the worst that could happen if you talked to the professor?"

From the kitchen, the three siblings hear, "Dinner is ready."

While walking into the kitchen, Megan says to Beau, "Don't think you get out of my question this easy."

Mom asks with curiosity, "What question, Beau?"

When no response was forthcoming from Beau, Megan repeats her questions, "Is Beau going to allow one insecure TA to ruin his GPA? What's the worst that could happen if he talks to the professor?"

Dad says, "We've asked Beau the same questions. We didn't get an answer either."

Without hesitation, Mom suggests that the topic be postponed and discussed with their aunt would be joining them later that evening. The three siblings thought this a great suggestion. Aunt Barb, their mom's sister, was a Life Coach and had helped the kids through some very trying and troubling times growing up.

Later that evening, there were hugs all around when Aunt Barb arrives. Mom says to her sister, "The kids all have an obnoxious person they are dealing with in their lives right now. Take center stage, sis and help my kids through their dilemmas! Dad and I will be in the other room cleaning up the kitchen."

Each sibling describes their obnoxious person and difficult situation they find themselves in. "Oh, I love it," says Aunt Barb. "Real life. Not as easy as it looks!" The three kids laugh and agree.

"Let's see. Katherine, you are dealing with a man that wants to take credit for everything you do. Megan, you're dealing with a prima donna who thinks the world revolves around her, and Beau, you're dealing with someone that is jealous of your success. Have I got this right?"

All three shake their heads in agreement.

Aunt Barb adds, "And none of you have approached the authority figures in your scenarios."

Again, all three siblings shrug and agree with their aunt.

"Katherine, you're trying to decide if you want to quit, yet haven't talked to your boss, correct?" asks Aunt Barb.

"Correct," answers Katherine.

"And Megan, you feel the coach would not do anything even if you did talk to him, right?" Aunt Barb asks.

"Right," responds Megan.

Looking at Beau, Barb says, "And you don't want to be a whiner and talk to the professor, correct?"

Beau answers in the affirmative.

"So you all are victims, feel powerless and helpless, and feel as if there is no solution to your problems. Is that about it?"

The three were not so quick to respond. *Hmmm*, they thought. *Victims? Powerless? Helpless?* These are not normally feelings that any of them feel. They were taught to create their own future, to be the masters of their lives. They were taught discernment, wisdom, to think for themselves, and to make the best decisions they could with the information at hand.

After all three of them sat silent for a long while, thinking, Beau comments, "I can see where our situations could be interpreted as us being helpless. Could it also be about us not wanting to make waves?"

Aunt Barb responds, "Yes, I agree with you. Not wanting to make waves. Isn't that what the TA wants, to flatten out your waves? There's no power in a flat wave."

Beau sits quietly, thinking, trying to see Aunt Barb's perception. Hesitantly, Beau says, "So, when I don't do anything, the TA gets what he wants, which is to intimidate me. He then feels powerful because I am powerless. He wants me to feel intimidated."

Smiling, Aunt Barb says, "Bullies are insecure, powerless people. Not taking any action, the TA feels justified in the manner in which he treats you. This makes him feel powerful."

"Huh!" Beau exclaims. "I think I understand what you are saying."

Aunt Barb turns her attention to Megan and says, "The prima donna. By chance, is this one of your competitors? Do you compete in the same event?"

Switching gears, Megan looks back at Aunt Barb and says, "Yes. How did you know?"

"So, her behavior is off-putting and catches you off guard. Right?" asks Aunt Barb.

Thinking before responding, Megan then says, "I think so."

"Sweet Megan," says Aunt Barb. "You always think the best about everyone. You don't want to think that anyone has a mean bone in their body or that they would deliberately manipulate others."

Confused, Megan says, "I'm being manipulated?"

Finally, Aunt Barb sits down next to Katherine. "Katherine, you are a team player. You are creative. You are solution-driven. Do you think Bob could be taking advantage of these wonderful qualities of yours?"

Trying to digest everything that their aunt was saying, slowly Katherine says, "So, you feel that Beau is being bullied, Megan is being manipulated, and I am being taken advantage of?"

"Yes, children, I do," Aunt Barb says with compassion. "The three of you were very fortunate when it came to parents. You had two loving, supportive parents. This is very rare. Very rare. Most children have horrendous, painful childhood memories and are deeply scarred, scared, unhappy, and insecure."

Megan asks if that's what motivates other people's behavior.

"Well, in part, yes. Another part is also about their needs." Aunt Barb explains, "For example, Katherine, one of your basic needs is connection. Because of this need, Bob is able to take advantage of you. Beau, one of your basic needs is accomplishment. The TA is threatening to rob you of this need and thus is able to bully you."

"And me, I have a need for security and stability," Megan interjects. "Being a professional athlete doesn't lend itself to stability, so I look to my friends to provide some stability for me. Thus, because my friends are so important to me, Julie is able to manipulate me."

Katherine asks if they can all do some EFT Tapping together. Aunt Barb thinks this a great suggestion. Tapping together creates a synergy of energy that helps move us through difficult issues we may not be able to get through on our own.

Together they tap:
* Even though I am being bullied, manipulated, and taken advantage of, I totally and completely accept myself.
* Even though I'm not sure what to do about my situation, I totally and completely accept myself.
* Even though I feel powerless and helpless, I totally and completely accept myself.
* Even though I'm not sure what the best course of action is for myself, I totally and completely accept myself.

By now, the three siblings are getting very tired. After all, they traveled that day, and decide that sleep is what each one needs.

Before sending them off to their rooms, Aunt Barb mentions she will be back tomorrow for Thanksgiving and around all weekend. She would talk with each of them before they left to return to their homes.

As each sibling falls asleep, their aunt's words ricochet in their mind. *"Bullied." "Powerless." "Manipulated." "Helpless." "Taken advantage of."*

The family that cooks together, stays together is their mom's motto. So, early the next day, Thanksgiving, everyone is up early to prepare the food for all their cousins and aunts and uncles and a few best friends thrown in who have no family close by. Busy day. Lots of chopping, dicing, tossing, and mashing. Lots of laughter, chatter, and teasing as the day progresses.

At the appointed hour rolls around, the house fills up with warmth, love, and companionship. Everyone fills their empty tummies to maximum capacity, feeling fulfilled and satisfied from both the food and friendship.

Megan sits down next to Aunt Barb. "I think I have it figured out," she says as she smiles.

"Let's hear it," says Aunt Barb as she turns to face Megan.

"My lesson is to learn to be at the effect of myself. Not to be distracted by someone that does not have my best interest at heart." Thinking to figure out how to put into words the thoughts that had been swirling around in her head for the last twenty four hours, Megan slowly adds, "Julie is playing mind games with me to disempower me. And, it's been working. I am less effective at practice and as a result, I don't perform to my maximum ability in a meet."

Aunt Barb says, "Being a professional athlete, you will constantly be challenged with outside distractions. No matter how you perform, you will hear praise and criticism. When there can only be one winner..." Aunt Barb is saying when Megan jumps in and finishes her sentence, "... Psychological games will be played. Like Julie befriending me to just hurt me to disempower me because I am her main competition."

"I do believe this might be what's going on," concludes Aunt Barb and then asks, "The question is, how do you deal with this situation? What's the solution?"

"I've thought about this for the last twenty-four hours. It's not about ignoring Julie. That's just the opposite side of the same issue. I need to desensitize myself to Julie or anyone trying to distract me from fulfilling my potential. I need to learn to be at the effect of myself. I need to empower myself."

"I agree," says Aunt Barb.

Megan says, "The next step is for us to tap, to do some EFT so I can desensitize the emotional response to Julie. Can you help me before I leave?"

"You bet ya! Would love to do some tapping with you," says a happy Aunt Barb.

The next day, Aunt Barb stops by early in the morning. Katherine is an early riser, the only one up as Aunt Barb walks into the kitchen. "So glad you stopped by, Aunt Barb. I think I have made some decisions about my job and how to deal with Bob."

"Want to share?" asks Aunt Barb.

"I was hoping you would ask. You're right. Bob is taking advantage of my connection need and my always wanting to be of assistance to others. When we have meetings with the boss, it's always the two of us together meeting with him. Most of the time, Bob starts talking before I have a chance to say anything," says Katherine.

Aunt Barb adds, "And you are too polite to interrupt Bob for fear that it might come off as you abusing and overpowering Bob."

"Exactly!" exclaims Katherine.

"What's the solution? Is it quitting your job; a job you love?" asks Aunt Barb.

Katherine takes a deep breath then says, "I do love my job. I do love the work I am doing. I'm not going to quit. I do need to handle the situation differently, though."

"How can you do that, handle the situation differently?" asks Aunt Barb.

Katherine answers, "I need to separate out the different responsibilities that Bob and I have. Each of us will have our own projects to work on instead of 'teamwork.' Thus, when there are meetings with the boss, each of us will report on the tasks that we each have worked on."

"Will the temptation be for you to help Bob accomplish his tasks," an inquiring aunt asks.

"I know where you are going. Changing the situation does not resolve the issue. And we both know the answer is 'Yes. I will be tempted to help Bob with his tasks.' And before you ask again, 'What's the solution?' I have an answer."

"Ah," a happy aunt says, "my flock is learning."

"We need to tap so there is no temptation. Resisting temptation is not resolving the problem. I need to allow others to sink or swim on their own efforts without the temptation of jumping in and 'saving' them! Hard lesson for me to learn," says an insightful Katherine.

"So, the problem isn't Bob?" asks Aunt Barb.

"Well, Bob is taking advantage of my weakness to help others. The problem with Bob is he doesn't want to look incompetent, so he takes credit for my accomplishments. My problem is that I am allowing him to do so," says Katherine.

"So," says Aunt Barb, waiting for Katherine to finish the sentence.

"So…" says Katherine thinking, "…my role in this situation is wanting to help and then allowing others to take credit for my work. If I didn't have these 'issues,' the scenario at work would be totally different."

Aunt Barb smiles and says, "And the solution is?"

"What a tease you are, Aunt Barb," Katherine remarks. Then she adds, "The solution is to tap so that I will not be tempted to rescue, or play teacher, or do the work myself. The solution is to tap so that I will stand up for myself and the work that I have accomplished."

"Would love to tap with you before you leave on Sunday," says a very exuberant aunt.

"You must have said something that made Aunt Barb very happy, Katherine," Beau says sleepily as he shuffles into the kitchen.

"Well," starts Katherine. Glancing over to Aunt Barb, she says, "I've decided not to quit my job and, instead, resolve the problems I have. Aunt Barb and I are going to do some tapping before I leave." Feeling cheerful and at peace, Katherine picks up her orange juice and wanders out to the garden to enjoy the warm sunshine that is rarely seen in the Northwest.

"Good morning, Aunt Barb," says Beau. "You're up early. The house is so quiet after all the chaos of Thanksgiving yesterday."

"Living in the neighborhood, I saw the kitchen light was on as I was out walking this morning and knew that someone was up."

"I'm glad you wondered in," says Beau.

"Oh," says an intrigued aunt.

"Yup. I've been thinking of what you said the other night. I'm not used to feeling disempowered or told I might be acting powerless and helpless," says Beau. "I think if anyone else had said that to me, I would not have taken them seriously and discounted the comments. But, I respect your knowledge, wisdom, and expertise."

"Thank you, Beau. Such a sweet compliment," says a happy Barb.

"The only time in my life that I have felt 'disempowered' is with this TA. I don't want to come across being a bully, but you say this is what is happening to me. You are right that I do feel helpless to change the situation in anyway. I've tried talking to the TA, reasoning with him, asking him how I could ace the multiple choice questions if I didn't know the material." With a heavy sigh, Beau opens the refrigerator, takes out a bottle of water and sits down next to Aunt Barb.

"You're right. I do feel stuck between a rock and a hard spot without a solution in sight. I talked with both Katherine and Megan yesterday and both seem to have resolved and solved their obnoxious-person situations. Megan thought her lesson was not to allow herself to be distracted by what is going on around her and concentrate on herself. Katherine thought that her lesson was to allow others to make their own mistakes without feeling like she needs to rescue someone that is struggling."

As Beau twists the cap off the water, he thoughtfully adds, "I'm stuck, Aunt Barb. I'm not sure what my lesson is. You thought I was being bullied by the TA. It's difficult for me to admit that I am being bullied by a wimp."

Cautiously, Aunt Barb asks, "Do you feel the TA is a bully in this situation?"

"Ah, clever, Aunt Barb," says Beau. "You taught me to listen to words. Because it is difficult for me to admit that I am being bullied, you ask if the TA is being a bully in my situation." Laughing, Beau says, "Okay. Yes, the TA is being a bully and I am being bullied." Making a grimacing face, Beau says, "Ouch!"

Together, they both laugh. Aunt Barb asks Beau what lesson he was learning. Beau questioningly responds, "How to deal with wimps that bully?"

"That works for me," says Aunt Barb. Then she asks Beau, "What's the solution?"

"I don't know, Aunt Barb. You have taught us that bullies are insecure; that if you stand up to a bully they usually stand down. How do I stand up to a bully and not come across as being a bully myself?"

"Excellent question. Have you figured out the lesson that you could be learning?" asks Barb.

Beau stands up and looks out into the garden, watching Katherine enjoying the sunshine. Turning around, leaning against the window ledge, Beau slowly says, as if thinking through his answer, "With both Katherine and Megan, I think they said something about two sides of the same issue and it wasn't about ignoring the situation." Pausing to take a sip of water, Beau then continues, "So, rather than get sucked into the situation, they needed to desensitize the emotions they had to the situations so that they would not be triggered again by similar circumstances. Did I get that right?" asks Beau.

"Ah, good student!" says a delighted Barb. "Even though we are aware of a situation, it doesn't mean a situation will change. In order for change to happen, we have to recognize, acknowledge, and take ownership of the situation before we can change," says Barb.

"So, you have been asking me questions to see if I recognize and acknowledge what's going on. Have I taken ownership yet?" asks Beau with a twinkle in his eye.

"Beau," starts Barb, "the world is full of people that are bitter and unhappy. They may smile and put on a friendly façade, but they will stab you in the back to bring you down. They are those that never take responsibility, always playing the victim. Nothing is ever their fault."

Beau says, "I'm with you so far."

Barb continues, "The world is full of the drama kings and queens that thrive on conflict and turmoil. And there are also the judges and critics that can be mean and cruel."

Walking over to the refrigerator, Beau pulls out another water and hands it to Aunt Barb. "You have been talking a lot this morning and I feel our talk isn't done. Have some water."

Appreciative of the gesture and indeed in need of water, Aunt Barb unscrews the cap and takes a few sips.

Beau says, "So, I think the point you are making is that my TA is all of the above. Bitter, victim, drama king, and a harsh critic all rolled into one."

Barb says with satisfaction, "The recognition stage."

"Yup," Beau says. "I do recognize and acknowledge that my TA is all four, but how do I take ownership of something that someone else is?"

"Excellent question. What's the answer?" asks Aunt Barb.

"Well, you have always said we can't take ownership of something that is not ours and we can't change anyone else. They have to make those decisions for themselves. I can only change me," Beau says.

"Agree. We can only change ourselves. What is it that you need to take ownership of?" asks Aunt Barb again.

Watching Megan join Katherine in the garden, Beau smiles, turns around to face Aunt Barb and says, "I have to take ownership of the way in which I **respond** to the TA, feeling powerless, helpless, and that nothing I do or say makes any difference to him." Chuckling, Beau asks, "Did I do good?"

"You did great," Aunt Barb says while smiling back at Beau.

"Okay, so the next question you will ask me is have I taken ownership of my response to the TA. And before you ask, I will answer in the 'affirmative,' professor. Yes, I have taken ownership of feeling powerless and helpless. Wow, that was hard to admit!" exclaims Beau.

"Beau," asks Aunt Barb with some levity, "now that you have taken ownership of your behavior, what's the solution?"

Walking over to the cabinet, Beau pulls out a few energy bars and says, "I think I will need some energy for this part of the conversation." He places the different choices on the counter in front of Aunt Barb so she can snack on whichever one she likes.

"So, what's the solution?" Beau says with a happy feeling. Taking ownership, he feels more hopeful and positive than he has felt all semester about this situation. "Well, conversing with the TA led nowhere. The professor always says his door is open to his students wanting to learn. I could talk with the professor." Then with a shy grin he says, "I know. I know what you are going to say. Megan and my parents have all wanted me to talk to the professor. It just didn't feel right to do so before this."

Picking up another energy bar, Barb asks Beau what he would say to the professor.

"Well, I'm not sure," Beau says. "I don't want to go to him to complain. I don't want it to seem like I'm whining about the TA. And, I don't want it to seem like I am asking for special treatment."

"Hmmm," says Barb. "Seems like you're in an awkward position with the professor. Switch places with the professor. You be him and have a student come to you with the same issues you are having with the TA. If you were the professor, how would you want to be approached?"

"Okay. That's an interesting idea," says Beau. To think, he walks back to the window to watch his sisters and speculates what Katherine would want if she was the professor. Aunt Barb munches on her energy bar while Beau formulates his answer. He imagined himself as the professor and what he would want to hear and not hear.

Looking back at Aunt Barb, Beau begins by explaining that he imagined Katherine as the student and himself as the professor and what they would want to hear and not hear. "I think I would not want to hear someone complain, make excuses, ask for special treatment. I guess I would have respect for the student that comes in wanting to know what they could do to raise their grade, do better, discover what they are missing or not understanding."

Aunt Barb is impressed and tells Beau she likes his answer. "Pretend I am your professor. What would you say?"

"Oh, role play. I'm me and you are the professor?" asks Beau.

"So, son what can I do for you?" says Barb with a husky voice, imitating a man.

"Sir," says Beau, as if he is speaking to his professor. "On the quizzes and multiple choice questions, I do very well. On the essays and papers, my scores are quite low, the lowest I have even received in college. Before the semester ends, I would like to understand what I might be missing that my scores are so low? How can I improve? Is there any way I can do some extra work to improve my grade?"

Beaming from ear to ear, Barb walks over Beau and gives him a hug. "I am proud of you."

Confused, Beau asks, "Were you my professor or aunt just then? My professor did not just hug me, right?" Both of them laugh. Hearing laughter, Megan and Katherine decide to investigate.

Once all three siblings were in the kitchen with their aunt, she says, "As much as we would like only pleasant, cheerful, loving people in our lives, this is not always possible. We are not cheerful and loving 100% of the time. We can be difficult at times as well. Learning to deal with obnoxious people, learning to detach, learning not to make and take everything personal are valuable tools."

Katherine says, "And that's where EFT Tapping comes in."

Megan adds, "EFT Tapping can transform the dysfunctional beliefs and desensitize the painful emotions. See? I **was** listening to you yesterday."

Then Beau adds, "Once the dysfunctional beliefs have been transformed and the painful emotions desensitized, our perception is improved, our mental thinking is improved, we are better able to make informed decisions, we don't take everything personally, our health is not negatively impacted, our heart doesn't beat 100 times/minute, smoke stops coming out of our ears, and our faces don't turn red with anger and frustration."

Laughing at the three siblings, Barb says, "I guess you have heard me say this a few times over the years."

Giving his aunt a huge hug, Beau says, "Aunt Barb, it just wasn't with our parents we lucked out. We lucked out, always having you around to counsel us, process us, and teach us the tools to handle life, particularly when it gets stressful. Aunt Barb and EFT Tapping are synonymous with love and gratitude."

"Thank you, kids," Barb says, a few tears filling her eyes. I'll tap with each of you separately before you leave for your homes and then I expect full reports from all three of you. Deal?"

In unison, the three say, "Deal."

Epilogue:

Email from Katherine to Aunt Barb:

Aunt Barb,

Thank you for, once again, coming to my rescue. I returned to work a different person with renewed energy and excitement. A few days after returning home, the owner (my boss) called me into his office for a one-on-one meeting. I thought maybe I might be let go. Instead, he praised me, gave me a huge Christmas bonus, and wanted to make sure I wasn't going to quit. He knew Bob wasn't pulling his weight, that I was doing the bulk of the work, and he wanted me to know he recognizes my value to the success of the company.

I feel so empowered by my boss. I've stepped up my game and involvement with the company and feel very positive about the future.

We did luck out having you for an aunt. Between you and EFT Tapping, I was able to turn my rescuing habit into a thing of the past.

Bob and I have restructured our roles by dividing tasks. I guess I was so busy rescuing Bob I never realized how much he had learned. He is now pulling his fair of the weight. He's happier. I'm happier. And my boss is certainly happier.

Guess the change had to start with me and my attitude. After tapping, the veil of frustration that clouded the true reality lifted, the three years of resentment dissolved, and I was able to see our relationship in a whole new light.

I am soooooo happy. Thank you!

Katherine

Email from Megan to Aunt Barb:

Aunt Barb,

You will not believe what happened when I returned to practice.

Julie tried to do her usual distraction number on me and it didn't work! She got so bored with me because I was really enjoying the entertainment she was providing for me. Since her "charms" didn't work on me any longer, she "selected" a new target to focus her destruction on.

The tapping helped me to regain myself. Julie is no longer annoying as she used to be. I no longer get sucked into her web of narcissism. She is who she is and that will never change.

After being back home for a week, the coach approached me and congratulated me on learning how to focus even though distractions are always around us. He said he didn't do anything about Julie because he knew that in order for me to be great I had to learn how to deal with Julie. He said I could handle everything else this sport might throw in my path to the winner's podium if I could handle my own teammate trying to sabotage me.

Cool, huh! Thanks Aunt Barb. You're the best!

Megan

Email from Beau to Aunt Barb:

Aunt Barb,

The last month has been a whirlwind with finals and I haven't had the time to email an update. Today was my last final. Writing this email is the first task I am accomplishing now that the semester is over.

The week after Thanksgiving, I did talk to my professor. I approached it as we had practiced. He pulled up my scores on his computer and found it interesting that I did well on the quizzes and test questions that were multiple choice and did not do well on the essay questions or my papers.

He then asked me questions. I felt like I was taking an oral exam. At the end of our conversation and oral examination, he smiled and said I indeed knew the material. He said to consider the oral exam as extra credit and added an A for that extra credit.

I also aced the final and the final even had essay questions! I haven't seen the TA or talked to him since returning from Thanksgiving. I do know the TA graded the exams.

I don't know if the professor told him of my visit or what may have influenced the way in which he graded my exam. And, I really don't care. This course and this semester is over.

Big hug coming your way when I get home for the holidays. Thank you (and EFT Tapping) for helping me feel more empowered. Proof is in the results.

Beau

Chapter 31
Tapping for Disappointments and Regrets

To move forward without pulling along all our baggage that is weighing up down, we need to heal the disappointments, regrets, and painful memories that tie us to the past.

Rule #1 for writing EFT Tapping statements is to use our own words. Rule #2 is process the emotions before beliefs. Below are tapping examples for disappointments, regrets, and painful memories.

TAPPING FOR DISAPPOINTMENT

JOANNE'S STORY

I thought my life would have turned out different than it did. I thought I would have been voted Teacher of the Year. When I graduated from college with my teaching degree, I was so excited to get into the classroom to shape young minds and add value to their lives as they grew and matured.

Have you been on a high school campus lately? When I was in high school, we didn't have cell phones, computers, texting, email, twitter, or snapchat. We talked to our fellow students, to the teachers. Our lives revolved around school, studying, learning, getting good grades to get into a good college.

Today, as teachers, we are competing with social media influencers, popstars, pro athletes, and seductive ad campaigns by large corporations. Teachers are last on the students' lists of people they want to receive advice from. The kids today think they know it all and nothing a teacher says has any impact.

My goal of being able to mold young minds is not a possibility with the kids of today. I could say something of value every day. The student would not hear it. If a popstar said the same thing, it is heard.

I know I shouldn't take and make it personal, but I end up disappointed that a popstar has more value to them than someone that is in the classroom with them every day attempting to prepare them for the "real world."

Between movies, tv shows, youtube videos, reality shows, these young kids of 14, 15, and 16 years of age, think they are wise and know everything. Life experience is not required.

I am burnt out. I don't want to be a teacher any longer but I am not qualified to do anything else. I don't know what else I would want to do. I am not independently wealthy or nearing retirement age. If I did retire, I would outlive my savings.

I am disappointed, frustrated, angry, sad, and afraid.

I am safe inside my comfort zone, but not happy. I'm too old to start another career and the career I have isn't fulfilling.

My life did not turn out as I imagined it would. I was so full of hope and excitement when I graduated from college. At the top of my class, I might add! And now as a teacher, I am ignored by my students, disregarded as having any value to and for them, and I'm too scared to try a different profession. There is no guarantee if I did switch professions I would be any happier than I am now. I know I am not happy now. What if I switched to a new profession and hated it even more than I do teaching?

Catch 22. Between a rock and hard spot. Lose-lose. That's my life. My life did not turn out as I thought it would.

First, we can do the round robin, eight statements/round of tapping. This will desensitize the emotions. Once the emotions are desensitized, we can look at the beliefs that need to be addressed. As we do the round robin, there will be a shift toward the end to begin reframing the disappointment and create a spark that maybe a different path could be possible to heal the disappointment.

The eight tapping points:
EB – Eyebrow
T – Temple
UE – Under the eye
UN – Under the nose
UL – Under the lips
CB – Collar bone
UA – Under the arm
TH – Top of the head

The Round Robin for this teacher's disappointment could look like this:

EB – I thought my life would have turned out
T – much different that it did.
UE – I thought I would have been
UN – voted Teacher of the Year.
UL – When I graduated from college
CB – I was so excited to get into the classroom
UA – to shape young minds and
TH – add value to their lives as they grew and matured.

EB – Have you been on a high school campus lately?
T – When I was in high school, we didn't have cell phones,
UE – computers, texting, email, twitter, or snapchat.
UN – We talked to our fellow students,
UL – to the teachers.
CB – Our lives revolved around school,
UA – studying, learning, getting good grades
TH – to get into a good college.

EB – Today, as teachers,
T – we are competing with
UE – social media influencers, popstars, pro athletes,
UN – and seductive ad campaigns by large corporations.
UL – Teachers are last on the students' list of people
CB – they want to receive advice from.
UA – The kids today think they know it all
TH – and nothing that a teacher says has any impact.

EB – My goal of being able to mold young minds
T – is not a possibility with the kids of today.
UE – I could say something of value every day,
UN – the students would not hear it.
UL – If a popstar said the same thing, it is heard.
CB – I know I shouldn't take and make it personal,
UA – but I end up disappointed that a popstar has more value to them
TH – than someone that is in the classroom with them every day.

EB – Between movies, tv shows, youtube videos, reality shows,
T – these young kids of 14, 15, and 16 years of age,
UE – think they are wise and know everything.
UN – Life experience is not required.
UL – I am burned out.
CB – I don't want to be a teacher any longer
UA – but I am not qualified to do anything else.
TH – I don't know what else I would want to do.

EB – I am not independently wealthy
T – nor nearing retirement age.
UE – If I did retire, I would outlive my savings.
UN – I am disappointed, frustrated, angry, sad, and afraid.
UL – I am safe inside my comfort zone, but not happy.
CB – I'm too old to start another career and the career I have isn't fulfilling.
UA – My life did not turn out as I imagined it would.
TH – I was so full of hope and excitement when I graduated from college.

EB – As a teacher, I am ignored by my students,
T – disregarded as having any value to and for them,
UE – and I'm too scared to try a different profession.
UN – There is no guarantee that if I did switch professions
UL – that I would be any happier than I am now.
CB – I am not happy now.
UA – What if I switched to a new profession
TH – and hated it even more than I do teaching?

EB – Catch 22.
T – Between a rock and hard spot.
UE – Lose-lose.
UN – That's my life.
UL – My life did not turn out as I thought it would.
CB – What if I could change the outcome?
UA – What if I could be happy in another profession?
TH – Am I cheating myself if I don't try?

EB – I'm not happy now so
T – it would seem anything could be better
UE – than the unhappiness I feel now.
UN – Maybe it is possible to go back to school
UL – or look into switching professions.
CB – There is nothing for me to lose
UA – if I started to look around,
TH – to do some research.

EB – Since my happiness is up to me
T – I have a choice.
UE – I can continue to feel sorry for myself
UN – or turn my disappointments into
UL – a win-win for me.
CB – I'm not even sure what a win-win would be
UA – since it's been so long since I have felt
TH – like a person of value, a winner.

EB – Since I do have choice
T – I think I would rather reach for something better.
UE – I know it will take me out of my comfort zone.
UN – When I graduated from college
UL – and became a teacher
CB – that pushed me out of my comfort zone.
UA – I think I can do it again.
TH – I think I can move out of my comfort zone.

After tapping the round robin to desensitize and reframe the disappointment, there might be some statements that did not clear and could be a belief. For those statements, we do one statement/round of tapping.

The statements for this teacher that did not clear and were beliefs were:

* Teachers are last on students' list of people to listen to.
* Kids today think they know it all.
* Nothing a teacher says has impact.
* It's not possible to mold the minds of kids today.
* I have no value to my students.
* My students treat me as if I have no value to them.
* A popstar has more influence over my students than I do.
* I would outlive my savings if I retired today.
* I am disappointed, frustrated, angry, sad, and afraid.
* I'm safe inside my comfort zone.
* It's not safe outside my comfort zone.
* I'm too old to start another career.
* The career I have isn't fulfilling.
* My life did not turn out as I imagined it would.
* I am ignored by my students.
* I'm too scared to try a different profession.

After Joanne tapped, she decided to explore different options of potential career paths. She was offered a position as a tutor, an instructor with an online school, and working with a motivational speaker that gives talks at high schools all over the United States.

Having a love of travel, she decided on working with the motivational speaker, helping her draft speeches and ghost writing her books.

Tapping for Regrets

Regrets differ from disappointments in that disappointment are more about the outcome whereas regrets are more about the choices we made that contributed to the dissatisfying outcome.

Regrets can also prevent us from moving forward, particularly if the result of our poor decisions resulted in trusting ourselves less than before.

Tapping our regrets will help to desensitize the emotions and reveal the beliefs that led to the decisions we made that left us feeling regretful.

Roger's Story

I met a wonderful woman our junior year in college. We lived together our senior year. With graduation nearing, we talked about our future. She wanted to get married and eventually start a family. I was ambivalent about having a family and being a father. I loved her and wanted to marry her. For me, she was the "one."

We each were offer jobs, but not within 1,000 miles of each other. She decided since I was ambivalent about a family, she would take the job offered her. I accepted the job that was offered to me.

We tried the long distance relationship thing. After several months, she ended the relationship since I was still ambivalent about having a family. If absence didn't make the heart grow fonder, she didn't think maintaining the relationship would change anything.

I did love her and I wanted to be with her and marry her but I still didn't know about being a parent.

Ten years have passed and I am still single. I have dated and have been in several serious relationships. When women start to talk about marriage, I back away. The relationships usually end soon after.

Ten years ago guys didn't go to counseling and talk about their feelings. Even today, I would feel ill at ease talking to someone about my feelings.

Women tend to think I am commitment phobic since I am still single in my thirties. I don't know if I am. I don't know if the reason I have not married is because I am commitment-phobic or ambivalent about being a father. I don't know if I am still single because I lost the love of my life and I don't think I can feel that way about someone else. I don't know if I have not moved on because I am still grieving the loss of that relationship.

I'm confused and have not been able to move forward in my life nor know how to figure out the cause of my inability to move forward.

Am I afraid of commitment? Is the reason I have not married is because I don't know if I want to be a father or afraid of commitment? Have I not moved forward because I am still grieving what I lost ten year ago? Or have I not moved on with my life because I am not willing to make a commitment?

My biggest regret is not seeking counseling ten years ago when I was with the love of my life.

My biggest regret is I did not seek out the answers to be able to move forward with my life. My biggest regret is I have been going round and round in the same cramped space for ten years. I do want to marry. I can't seem to get there from here.

Roger used EFT Tapping to desensitize the emotions and his confusion that helped him to move forward with his life.

Using his words, we can script EFT Tapping statements, and then look more closely at the statements that did not clear, and make them into tapping statements.

The tapping could look like this (using his own words):

EB – I met a wonderful woman our junior year in college.
T – We lived together our senior year.
UE – With graduation nearing,
UN – we talked about our future.
UL – She wanted to get married
CB – and eventually start a family.
UA – I was ambivalent about having a family
TH – and being a father.

EB – I loved her
T – and wanted to marry her.
UE – For me, she was the "one."
UN – We each were offer jobs but
UL – not within 1,000 miles of each other.
CB – She decided since I was ambivalent about a family,
UA – she would take the job offered her.
TH – I accepted the job that was offered to me.

EB – We tried the long distance relationship thing,
T – but after several months,
UE – since I was still ambivalent about having a family,
UN – she ended the relationship.
UL – If absence didn't made the heart grow fonder,
CB – she didn't think maintaining the relationship
UA – would change anything.
TH – I don't know.

EB – I did love her
T – I wanted to be with her
UE – and marry her.
UN – I still didn't know about being a parent.
UL – Ten years later,
CB – I am still single.
UA – I have dated
TH – and have been in

EB – several serious relationships.
T – When women start to talk about marriage,
UE – I back away. The relationships
UN – usually end soon after.
UL – Ten years ago, guys didn't go to counseling
CB – and talk about their feelings.
UA – I would feel ill at ease talking to someone
TH – about my feelings even today.

EB – Women tend to think I am commitment phobic,
T – since I am still unmarried in my thirties.
UE – I don't know if I am.
UN –I don't know if the reason I have not married is
UL – because I am commitment phobic
CB – or ambivalent about being a father.
UA – I don't know if I am still single
TH – because I loss the love of my life

EB – and I don't think I can feel
T – that way about someone else.
UE – I don't know if I have not moved on because
UN – I am still grieving the lost of that relationship.
UL – I'm confused
CB – and have not been able to move forward in my life
UA – nor know how to figure out the cause
TH – of my inability to move forward.

EB – Am I afraid of commitment?
T – Is the reason I have not married is because
UE – I don't know if I want to be a father
UN – or afraid of commitment?
UL – Have I not moved forward because
CB – I am still grieving what I lost ten year ago?
UA – Or have I not moved on
TH – with my life because I am

EB – not willing to make a commitment?
T – My biggest regret is that
UE – I did not seek counseling ten years ago
UN – when I was with the love of my life.
UL – My biggest regret is
CB – I did not seek out the answers
UA – to be able to move forward with my life.
TH – My biggest regret is that I have been

EB – going round and round
T – in the same cramped space for ten years.
UE – I do want to be married.
UN – I can't seem to get there from here.
UL – I don't know if there is a solution.
CB – I don't know if it is possible for me
UA – to move beyond the cramped space
TH – I limit myself to.

EB – I would like to think it's possible
T – to find a solution
UE – to be able to move forward with my life.
UN – I would like to think it is possible for me
UL – to love someone without reservation.
CB – I would like to be able to marry some day.
UA – I would like to know the reason
TH – I have stayed stuck.

EB – I think I should try to find solutions.
T – I think I should try to find a therapist
UE – that can help me find the answers I seek.
UN – It might be uncomfortable
UL – but remaining single is even
CB – more uncomfortable. I think I'm ready now
UA – to move beyond the cramped box
TH – I have lived in for ten plus years.

For Roger, the tapping started with the regret and confusion. The tapping ended with the possible of reframing being stuck to considering moving out of the cramped box he felt he had existed in for the last ten years.

Once he was able to desensitize the situation and the regrets, the statements that didn't clear can be used as tapping statements, one statement for the complete round of tapping, all eight points.

The additional statements he tapped were:

* I was ambivalent about having a family.
* I back away from a relationship when a woman starts to talk about marriage.
* Others think I am commitment phobic.
* I don't know if I am still single because I lost the love of my life.
* I am still grieving the lost of the relationship with the love of my life.
* I am afraid of making a commitment to marriage.
* I am afraid of making a commitment to being a father.
* My biggest regret is that I did not seek counseling ten years ago.
* My biggest regret is I did not seek out the answers ten years ago.
* I don't know how to get from here to there in regards to marriage.

After tapping, Roger realized he wasn't commitment phobic. He wanted to be married, but did not want to be a father. Once he was clear on want he did and did not want, his relationships shifted towards women that also wanted to be married but not have children.

Within two years of this tapping assignment, Roger proposed and is happily married.

Books by Tessa Cason

All Things EFT Tapping Manual

* Why does EFT Tapping work for some and not for others?
* How do you personalize EFT Tapping to be most effective for you?
* What is the very first tapping statement you need to tap?

This manual provides instructions on how to heal our disappointments, regrets, and painful memories.

EFT Tapping information has instructions on what to do if a tapping statement does not clear, what to do if tapping doesn't work for you, and how to write your own tapping statements.

We must eliminate the dysfunctional beliefs if we want to make changes in our lives. EFT Tapping can do just that. EFT Tapping is a simple, yet very powerful tool to heal our beliefs, emotions, painful memories, and stories.

500 EFT Tapping Statements for Moving Out of Survival

Survival is stress on steroids. It's feeling anxious and not good enough. Survival may be the most important topic we can heal within ourselves. Survival is programmed into our DNA.

Ella returned home from the market with her three year old daughter to find a note from her husband that he did not want to be married any longer. Under the note were divorce papers, the number of the divorce attorney, and $500.

Wanting to be able to give her daughter a wonderful childhood, she had to figure out how to survive and thrive. This is her story and the tapping statements she tapped.

Dr. John Montgomery says, "All 'negative,' or distressing, emotions, like fear, disgust, or anxiety, can be thought of as 'survival-mode' emotions: they signal that our survival and well-being may be at risk."

80 EFT Tapping Statements for Change

If it is not okay or safe for our lives to change, every time our lives change, the body is subjected to a tremendous amount of stress.

After graduating from high school, Charlie's dad told Charlie he could continue to live at home, but he would be charged room and board. At 18, Charlie was now financially responsible for himself. He was able to find a job and moved out.

Within a year, circumstances forced Charlie to move back home. Day after day, Charlie rode the bus to work. After work, he rode the bus home. One day as Charlie was riding the bus to work, he noticed another regular rider, Dan, tapping his head.

Together Dan and Charlie began tapping. Find out the results of their tapping and the statements they tapped.

300 EFT Tapping Statements for Self-defeating Behaviors, Victim, Self-pity

Tom had lots of excuses and reasons for his lack of "results." His boss, Robert MacGregor, saw the potential Tom had and asked his longtime friend, Sam Anderson, a life coach, to work with Tom. Read Tom's story to understand how Tom was able to step into his potential.

Self defeating behaviors take us away from our goals, from what we want, leaving us feeling exhausted, disempowered, and defeated. Self defeating thoughts are the negative thoughts we have about ourselves and/or the world around us such as "I'm not good enough", "I have to be perfect to be accepted."

Most likely, you have tried to change the self-defeating and self sabotage behavior, yet here you are with the same patterns.

100 EFT Tapping Statements for Feeling Fulfilled

John wasn't sure what would fulfill him. He loved his job and didn't want to find a new career, but he wasn't feeling fulfilled in his life. With the help of his wife, John found what would be fulfilling.

Fulfillment is a simple formula, actually. It's the follow-through that might be the problem.

What would prevent you from being fulfilled? Do you know what the blocks might be, the reason you remain out of sync, unfulfilled? Is it about leaving your comfort zone or maybe it's that you allow your limitations to define your life?

It is possible to remove the blocks, heal the beliefs on the subconscious level, and move toward your desire for fulfillment. To do so, we need a powerful tool. One such tool is EFT Tapping, the Emotional Freedom Technique.

100 EFT Tapping Statements for Being Extraordinary!

Accomplishing extraordinary performances, having incredible successes, or earning large sum of money does not equate to an extraordinary person. This book is about discovering your extraordinary character.

Extraordinary – Exceeding ordinary, beyond ordinary.

Extraordinary starts with the self, our character, depth and strength of our being. It's being congruent, walking our talk. It is the love, compassion, and tenderness we show ourselves. It's the pure and highest essence of our being.

Rebecca was approaching a time in her life in which she was doing some soul searching and examining her life. She didn't feel extraordinary. In her late 50s, she felt she was just ordinary. She reached out to Tessa. The email exchanges are included in this book along with tapping statements.

400 EFT Tapping Statements for Being Empowered and Successful

Being empowered is not about brute strength or the height of our successes. It is the strength, substance, and character of our inner being. It is knowing that whatever life throws at us, we will prevail.

Ava has just started a business with her two very successful sisters. She wants the business with her sisters to succeed, yet, she doesn't feel empowered. She doesn't want to feel as if the business would fail because of her and is ready to do the emotional work so she matches her sisters' power and success.

Sophie, Ava's roommate and an EFT practitioner-in-training, works with Ava. With Sophie's help, Ava begins to feel empowered and that her business with her sisters will be a success.

300 EFT Tapping Statements for Healing the Self

We live in a complex world with multiple influences. At birth, it starts with our parents and soon afterwards, the influence of other family members (grandparents, siblings, etc.), TV shows, cartoon characters, commercials, and peers. As we get older, we have the influences of teachers, coaches, tutors, television and movie stars, pop stars, sports heroes, and so many other.

When Pete was offered a promotion at work and was not excited about something he had worked so hard to accomplish, he knew he needed to find some answers. He thought he was living his mother's version of his life. He didn't know what brought him joy.

With the help of EFT and an EFT Practitioner, Pete was able to discover his version of his life, what brought him joy, and how to live a fulfilling life.

EFT Tapping for Anxiety, Fear, Anger, Self Pity, Courage (1,000 Tapping Statements)

Anxiety is a combination of 4 things: Unidentified Anger, Hurt, Fear, and Self Pity. We expect error, rejection, humiliation, and actually start to anticipate it.

When we are not in present time, we are either in the past or the future. Anger is the past. Fear is the future. Fear could actually be anger that we failed in the past and most likely will fail again in the future.

It takes courage on our part to heal the anxiety, identify the hurt, and to give up the self-pity. To heal, to thrive, and flourish, we need to address not only the Anxiety, but also the fear, anger, self pity, and hurt.

Healing is not about managing symptoms. It's about alleviating the cause of the symptoms.

80 EFT Tapping Statements for Feeling Less Than and Anxiety

Rene was excited for the year long mentoring program she enrolled in. *How wonderful*, she thought, *to be surrounded with like-minded people.* Five months into the program, she abruptly dropped out. Find out how her feeling Less Than and her Anxiety sabotaged her personal growth.

Anxiety has four parts: unidentified anger, hurt, fear, and self-pity. Living in a state of fear, we want a guarantee that our decisions and choices will produce the results or outcomes that we want. Feeling less than is played out in a cycle of shame, hopelessness, and self-pity. We feel shame about who we are, that we have little value, and that we are not good enough.

Feeling "less than" spirals down into depression, survival, and self-sabotage.

240 EFT Tapping Statements for Fear

Two months before school ended, Lennie was downsized from as a high school music teacher. When he was unable to find another job, fear crept into his thoughts. What if he couldn't find a job in music again? He wasn't qualified to do anything different. He was scared that he would not be able to support his family and they would end up homeless. He could feel the fear as his stomach was in knots.

Fear is that sense of dread, knots in the stomach, chill that runs down our spine, and the inability to breathe. We all know it. Fight-Flight-Freeze.

Fear is a self-protection mechanism. It is an internal alarm system that alerts us to potential harm. When we are in present time, we have the courage, awareness, wisdom, discernment, and confidence to identify and handle that which could cause us harm.

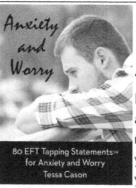

80 EFT Tapping Statements for Anxiety and Worry

"I just can't do this anymore," said Frank to his wife Mary. "You worry about everything. When we got married, your anxiety was something you did every now and then. But now you are paranoid about everything. I leave for work and you act like you are never going to see me again."

Anxiety is a combination of 4 things: unidentified anger, hurt, fear, self-pity. We expect error, rejection, humiliation, and actually start to anticipate it. It is an internal response to a perceived threat to our well-being. We feel threatened by an abstract, unknown danger that could harm us in the future.

Worry is a mild form of anxiety. Worry is a tendency to mull over and over and over anxiety-provoking thoughts. Worry is thinking, in an obsessive way, about something that has happened or will happen. Going over something again and again and asking, "What will I do? What should I have done?"

200 ET Tapping Statements for Healing a Broken Heart

She found someone who made her feel cherished, valued, and loved. Tall, dark, and handsome as well as aware, present and understanding. Matt was an awesome guy. He thought she, too, was someone special, intriguing, and awesome.

Matt was promoted at work which meant months away from home and thus, decided to end their relationship. Her best friend introduced her to EFT Tapping to heal her broken heart.

Time does not heal all. Healing the grief of a broken heart is not easy. Grief is more than sadness. Grief is a loss. Something of value is gone. Grief is an intense loss that breaks our hearts.

Over time, unhealed grief becomes anger, blame, resentment, and/or remorse. To heal a broken heart, we need to identify, acknowledge, and healed the dysfunctional beliefs. EFT Tapping can help.

400 EFT Tapping Statements for Dealing with Emotions

Did you see the movie Pleasantville with Tobey Maguire and Reese Witherspoon, two siblings who are trapped in a 1950s black and white TV show, set in a small midwest town where everything is seemingly perfect. David and Jennifer (Tobey and Reese) must pretend they are Bud and Mary Sue Parker, the son and daughter in the TV show.

Slowly, the town begins changing from black and white to color as the townspeople begin to experience emotions. Experiencing emotions is like adding color to a black and white movie. Color adds a depth, enjoyment, and pleasure to the movie. Emotions add depth, enjoyment, and pleasure to our lives.

Emotions add animation, richness, and warmth to our lives. They give our lives meaning and fullness. Without emotions, our lives would be as boring as watching a black and white movie.

80 EFT Tapping Statements for Abandonment

Feelings of abandonment can be triggered by the ending of a relationship as well as the death of an individual. Even though we may have an intellectual understanding of death, there is still a feeling of abandonment when someone we treasure dies. For a small child, they do not understand death. They may still expect the parent to return at any time.

Even though Kevin drove an expensive sports car he wasn't the playboy type. He wanted to settle down and start a family. Kevin felt Susan could be "the one." He wanted to talk to her about taking their relationship to the next level.

Before Kevin could talk to Susan, she ended the relationship because of his insecurities in their relationship. She felt it had to do with the abandonment of his mom when he was a child. This book gives you the exact statements that Kevin tapped to deal with his insecurities in relationships.

EFT Tapping Statements for A Broken Heart: Abandonment, Anger, Depression, Grief, Emotional Healing (1,000 Statements

Time does not heal all. When our hearts have been shattered, we feel nothing will ever be the same again. We are flooded with emotions... anger, grief, depression...

Regardless of what led to the broken heart, maybe a death, divorce, or a breakup, the result is the same...a broken heart. To heal a broken heart is not only about healing the grief, but also the feelings of abandonment, anger, and depression.

Being abandoned is a verb. It is something that "happens to us." The result of being abandoned is anger, grief, and depression. Grief is the sadness we experience when we have lost something of value.

In order to heal, we need to resolve the anger, grief, abandonment, and depression that resulted from our hearts being fractured.

200 ET Tapping Statements for Wealth

After graduating from high school, Amy looked for a job for a solid year unsuccessfully! She lacked the necessary experience and education. She felt like she was in a vicious cycle, going round and round and round. Finally, she was hired at a large chain store. For the last eight years, she has been shuffled, unhappily, between different departments.

As a birthday gift, her mom gave her a session with an EFT Practitioner to determine what she wanted to do with her life. Follow along with Amy on her journey to self-discovery.

What we manifest in our lives is a direct result of our beliefs. If we have a mentality of wealth and abundance, we will prosper and thrive.

Our beliefs determine the level of our wealth and abundance. To heal our dysfunctional beliefs, we need a powerful tool. EFT Tapping is one such tool.

EFT Tapping Statements for Prosperity, Survival, Courage, Personal Power, Success
(1,000 Statements)

What we believe determines our prosperity. Our beliefs determine our thoughts and feelings which in turn determine our choices and decisions. Therefore, what we manifest in our lives is a direct result of our beliefs. If we are happy and joyful, we will see happiness in everything. If we are fearful, we will see fear around every corner. If we have a mentality of abundance, we will prosper.

It is difficult to be prosperous when we are stuck in survival. In survival, we feel disempowered to thrive. We can only survive. It takes Courage to step into our Personal Power and to Succeed. We need a powerful tool to heal our dysfunctional beliefs. EFT Tapping is one such tool.

In this book, there are 200 tapping statements for each of these 5 topics - Prosperity, Survival, Courage, Personal Power, and Success.

80 EFT Tapping Statements for Abundance, Wealth, Money

Abby just had her 46th birthday. She tried to celebrate but she didn't have anything to be happy about. Her parents had died in a car accident the Christmas before while driving home from her new home after celebrating Christmas. Both of her parents were real estate agents. She was their transaction coordinator. The three of them had their own offices, handling any real estate transaction that someone might need. Without them, she had no real estate transactions to coordinate.

Abby funds were running dry. She had applied for jobs without success. Abby talked to every one she and her parents knew in hopes of finding a job. With the slow real estate market, she was unable to find any work.

Find out how Abby turned her life around and the exact statements that Abby tapped to deal with her monetary issues.

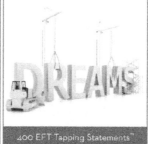

400 EFT Tapping Statements for Dreams to Reality

Have you done everything you were supposed to do for your dreams to become reality? You were clear on what they were. You made your vision boards with lots of pictures of what you desired. You visualized them coming true and living that life. You've stated your affirmations over and over and over for their fulfillment. You released and allowed the Universe to handle the details. And, now, dust is collecting on your vision boards and you are still waiting for the Universe to handle the details.

Our dreams are our hopes and desires of what we want to come true one day. They are snapshots of what we want our future to be. Yet, sometimes, maybe most of the time, our dreams do not become reality and never manifest themselves in our lives. We gave up on our dreams a long time ago.

Jane shares her story of how she used EFT Tapping to turn her dreams into reality.

300 ET Tapping Statements for Intuition

Quinn was one of Tessa's students in her Developing Your Intuition class. She had been hesitant to develop her intuition. One of her basic needs was Belonging. If she was intuitive, she might not belong and thus, realized this was part of her hesitation.

She also had a tendency to avoid which also wasn't conductive to developing her intuition. Tessa wrote out some EFT Tapping statements for her to tap:
* I ignore my inner voice.
* No one I know uses intuition.
* I'm too logical to be intuitive.
* Being intuitive is too complicated.

Included in this book are exercises and helpful hints to develop your intuition as well info on Symbolism, Colors, Number, Charkas, Asking Questions of Our Intuition, Archetypes, and 36 Possible Reasons We Took Physical Form.

Emotional Significance of Human Body Parts..Chasing the Pain

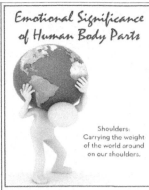

Shoulders: Carrying the weight of the world around on our shoulders.

"We carry the weight of the world around on our shoulders. The emotional significance of the shoulder is about responsibility.

The body "talks" to us...in its language. To understand what the body is saying, we need to learn the body's language.

Jona greeted me at the airport gate on crutches. After hugging each other, she asked what the left ankle meant. I told her the left side of the body had to do with what's going on in the inside and the ankles had to do with commitments.

She had been dating a man for the last two months and he just proposed.

Chasing the Pain is a technique with EFT Tapping that as we tap for a physical pain we are experiencing, the original pain might disappear only to be felt in a different part of the body.

100 EFT Tapping Statements for Accepting Our Uniqueness and Being Different

Brian was an intelligent high school student with average grades. He tested high on all the assessment tests. Brian didn't think of himself as intelligent since his grades were only average. He didn't plan on going to college because he thought he wasn't smart enough and would flunk out.

His counselor knew otherwise and suggested Brian retake the tests to see if the tests were wrong. Find out Brian's scores after he retook the tests and how Mr. Cole introduced EFT Tapping to Brian.

If you were your unique self, do you fear being alone, rejected, or labeled as "undesirable?" Or maybe it's being laughed at and ridiculed for being different and unique?

When we play our lives safe, we end up feeling angry, anxious, powerless, hopeless, and depressed.

Muscle Testing..Obstacles and Helpful Hints

Muscle testing is a method in which we can converse with the subconscious mind as well as the body's nervous system and energy field.

This book details 10 obstacle and 10 helpful hints to successfully muscle test.

One obstacle is that it is a necessity that the tester be someone that calibrates the same, or above, that of the testee, on David Hawkins' Map of Consciousness or be in the higher altitudes, 250 or higher, on the Map.

Helpful hint: When muscle testing, the tester and testee should not make eye contact with each other. With eye contact, the answer would be "our" energy instead of the "testee's" energy.

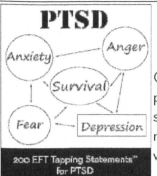

200 ET Tapping Statements for PTSD

George believed that if he prepared for his death, it was signaling the Universe he was ready to die. George did die without preparing his wife.

George took care of everything. The only thing Helen had to take care of George.

After George died, she had no idea if they owned the home they lived in, if George had life insurance, how to pay bills, if they had money, if they did, where was it? She didn't know if George had left a will. She was not prepared for George's death or how to take care of everything that George took care of.

With the help of friends and EFT Tapping, Helen was able to heal and learn how to take care of everything that George once did.

Healing is not about managing symptoms. It is about alleviating the cause of the symptoms.

EFT Tapping Statements for PTSD, Survival, Disempowered, Fear, Anger (1,200 Statements)

The potential exists for anyone that is in any life threatening situation in which they fear for their life, that believes death is imminent, to experience PTSD.

With PTSD, our Survival is at stake. As a result of our survival being threatened, we feel Disempowered to thrive. We can only survive. When we are caught in Survival, Fear is a prevalent emotion. When we feel Disempowered, Anger is just beneath the surface.

To heal, to thrive, and flourish, we need to address not only the PTSD, but also Survival and Feeling Disempowered, Fear, and Anger. (Thus, the 5 topics in this PTSD Workbook.)

Healing PTSD is a process in which we must desensitize, decrease, and heal the survival response. EFT Tapping is the best method to do so.

200 EFT Tapping Statements for Conflict

"Hi, Julia. So glad you called." Excitedly, I said, "I just finished decorating the house and I'm ready for Christmas!"

Not at all thrilled to be talking to her sister-on-law, Julia said, "That's why I'm calling. You don't mind if I host the family Christmas get-together, do you?"

A little surprised, I said, "Well, I do.

"Tough," she said. "I'm hosting Christmas this year."

This wasn't the first "conflict" with her sister-in-law. But, Audrey was a conflict coward and did not engage.

After EFT Tapping, Audrey overcame her issues with conflict. Find out how and who hosted Christmas that year!

80 EFT Tapping Statements for Anger

Doug was immensely proud of his son, Andy, until he watched his son (a high school senior) jeopardize his chance at an athletic scholarship to attend college. The count was 3-2, three balls and two strikes. The final pitch was thrown and Andy let it go by. The umpire shouts, "Strike!" Andy has just struck out.

"What's wrong with your eyes old man?" Andy shouts at the umpire. "That was a ball. It wasn't in the strike zone. Need instant replay so you can see it in slow motion? I'm not out!"

Andy, was following his father's example of being a rageaholic. EFT Tapping helped both Doug and Andy to take control of his life and his anger.

Anger is not right or wrong, healthy or unhealthy. It is the expression of anger that makes it right or wrong, healthy or unhealthy.

400 ET Tapping Statements for Being a Champion

Jack was a professional runner that injured himself at the US Championships. He was unable to compete at the World Championship. The previous year, Jack had won gold at the World Championships. After six months, he still was not able to run even though the doctors assured him he should be able to run. He had exhausted all medical and physical therapy treatments without success or hope of being able to run pain-free.

Our of frustration, Jack decided to look at the mental piece with a transformation coach. Follow Jack's recovery back to the track through EFT Tapping.

Champions are rare. If being a champion was easy then everyone would be a champion and a champion would not be anything special. It is in the difficulty of the task that, once accomplished, makes a champion great.

EFT Tapping Statements for Champion, Personal Power, Success, Self Confidence, Role Model (1,000 Statements)

Being a champion is more than just being successful. It is the achievement of excellence. It is more than just being competent. It is about stepping into one's power. It is more than just setting goals. It is the achievement of those goals with perseverance, dedication, and determination. It is not just about the practicing, training, and learning. It is the application and implementation of the training and learning into a competition and into everyday situations.

Champions are successful, but not all successful people are champions. Champions are powerful, but not all powerful people are champions. Champions are confident but not all confident people are champions. Champions dream big but not all people that dream big are champions.

300 EFT Tapping Statements for Dealing with Obnoxious People

Three siblings were each dealing with an obnoxious person in their lives. Katherine was dealing with a co-worker that took credit for her accomplishments.

Megan, a professional athlete, was distracted by a narcissistic team member that disrupted practice and thus, her performances at meets.

Peter was a very successful college student that had a Teaching Assistant jealous of everything that Peter was and the TA was not.

Read how each resolved and solved their issue with an obnoxious person.

80 EFT Tapping Statements for Self Esteem

Ron had driven a semi-trailer truck for 30 years for the same company. To celebrate his 60th birthday and 30 years of service his company had a celebration for him. After the celebration, Ron's boss suggested that he find a job that was more age appropriate. Ron's lack of self-esteem was interfering with moving on with his life. This book gives you the exact statements that Ron tapped to heal his lack of self esteem, self respect, and self-pride.

From birth to about the age of seven, we learn self love from mom. From about the age of seven through twelve, from dad we learn self esteem, earned loved Self esteem is about the feelings, respect, and pride we have in ourselves.

The lack of self esteem shows up in our lives as a lack self respect and/or pride in ourselves. This "lack" will taint every area of our lives.

340 ET Tapping Statements for Healing From the Loss of a Loved One

Grief is more than sadness. It is more than unhappiness. Grief is a loss. Something of value is gone. Grief is an intense loss that breaks our heart. Loss can be the death of a loved one, a pet, a way of life, a job, a marriage, one's own imminent death. Grief is real.

Over time, unhealed grief becomes anger, resentment, blame, and/or remorse. We become someone that we are not. It takes courage to move through the grief and all the emotions buried deep within.

John's father died of a heart attack while gardening. A year after his death, John still was not able to move on or be happy. His wife handed him a business card of an EFT Practitioner and recommended therapy to heal the grief. After working with the Practitioner, John was able to find his joy again.

100 EFT Tapping Statements for Feeling Deserving

Sarah, a sophomore in college, was unsure of what to declare as her major. She met with a guidance counselor who wanted to chat first.

Sarah thought of herself as an accident since she had two older siblings who had already moved out of the house when she was five. Her parents had been looking forward to an empty nest, instead, they had a third child that was just starting school.

Sarah had felt undeserving her whole life, even though her parents loved her dearly and never treated her life an accident.

Travel the path Sarah walked with the counselor to finally feel deserving.

200 EFT Tapping Statements for Procrastination. What I Want to Do and What I Have to Do

Procrastination is about avoiding.
* What are we avoiding?
* What are we afraid to find out?
* What are we not wanting to do?
* What are we not willing to face?

Is it:
* We don't have the tools and skills to do something.
* Rebellion
* Lack of motivation.
* Not knowing what needs to be done.
* Poor time management.

The list is long why we procrastinate and what it could be about. What do we do to heal our procrastination tendencies? EFT Tapping. To heal we have to be able to recognize, acknowledge, and take ownership of that which we want to heal. Then we have to delete the dysfunctional beliefs on the subconscious level. EFT is one such tool that can do just that.

80 EFT Tapping Statements for Relationship with Self

Stephanie, now 55 years old, used to be excited about life and about her life. That was 35 years ago. She was engaged to the love of her life. A month before the wedding her fiancée ran off with a beauty queen.

After 35 years, Stephanie still felt defeated, beaten, defective, broken, and flawed. She was still resentful. She had become comfortable in apathy because she did not know how to move beyond her self-pity.

With the help of EFT Tapping, Stephanie was able to heal her wounded self and begin to live life again.

Do you feel disconnected from yourself? Do you feel as if you could never be whole? Do you feel defeated by life? To change our lives, we have to be able to recognize, acknowledge, and take ownership of that which we want to change. Then heal the dysfunctional beliefs on a subconscious level. EFT Tapping can help.

700 ET Tapping Statements for Weight, Emotional Eating, & Food Cravings

Emma's sister's wedding was fast approaching. She would be asked at the wedding how her diet was going.

Emma has struggled with her weight for the last 35 years, since high school. Out of desperation, Hannah began working with an EFT Practitioner. Follow her journey to healing the cause of her weight issues.

Excess weight, food cravings, emotional eating, and overeating are symptoms of deeper unresolved issues beneath the weight. Attempting to solve the problem by only dealing with the symptoms is ineffective and does not heal the issue.

Weight is the symptom. The usual programs for weight loss aren't working because they are attempting to solve the problem by dealing with the symptom instead of healing the cause.

EFT Tapping Statements for Weight + Food Cravings, Anger, Grief, Not Good Enough, Failure (1,150 Statements)

Excess weight, food cravings, emotional eating, and overeating are symptoms of deeper issues beneath the weight. Attempting to solve the problem by only dealing with the symptoms is ineffective and does not heal the issue.

The usual programs for weight loss aren't working because they are attempting to solve the problem by dealing with the symptom instead of healing the cause.

IF WE WANT TO HEAL OUR WEIGHT ISSUES, WE NEED TO HEAL THE CAUSE...THE DYSFUNCTIONAL BELIEFS AND EMOTIONS.

HEALING IS NOT ABOUT MANAGING SYMPTOMS. IT'S ABOUT ALLEVIATING THE CAUSE OF THE SYMPTOMS.

80 EFT Tapping Statements for Addictions

Derrick's mom died when he was a senior in high school. His dad (an alcoholic) told Derrick that as soon as he graduated from high school, he was on his own.

The day that Derrick graduated from high school, he went down and enlisted in the army. In the army, he started to drink. A month after his enlistment concluded, he met a wonderful woman. They married and had a child.

One day when Derrick returned home from the bar, he found an empty house and a note. The note told him that since has unwilling to admit he was an alcoholic or to go to counseling, she was left with only one choice. That choice was to relocate herself and their daughter to some place safe, away from him.

Derrick felt he had nothing to live for. He discovered someone at work that was a recovering alcoholic. She introduced her secret, EFT Tapping, to Derrick.

80 EFT Tapping Statements for Weight and Emotional Eating

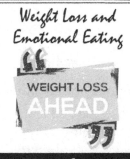

Excess weight is a symptom, not the cause of overeating and emotional eating.

The day that Tracy was graduating from UCLA, she received a phone call that her father had fallen and had been hospitalized. She was on the next flight home to Dallas. It was decided that her father needed surgery and that Tracy should stay on for a short while to care for her dad. No one asked Tracy what she wanted. But, she stayed anyway.

Seven months later, even though her father had mended, Tracy had become her father's caregiver. This is not what Tracy had planned to do with her life after graduating from college. Every month, over the course of the seven unhappy months, Tracy's weight spiraled up, until she was at her highest weight EVER.

This book gives you the exact statements that Tracy tapped to heal the cause of her weight gain.

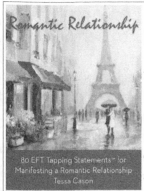

80 ET Tapping Statements for Manifesting a Romantic Relationship

Tanya tells the story about her best friend, Nica. Nica wants a relationship. She wants to be in love, the happily-ever-after kind of love. Nica is self-absorbed, self-centered, smart, and pretty.

Nica has had several long-term relationships but, never allows anyone close enough to get to know her. When she is in between boyfriends, she always whines:

* No man will ever want me.
* The odds are slim to none that I will find anyone.
* I have a bad track record with men so I give up.
* There will never be anyone for me.
* My desires will never be fulfilled.

Tanya is a tapper and finally Nica agrees to do some tapping as a last resort! The Tapping Statements that Nica tapped to manifest a relationship are listed in this eBook.

80 EFT Tapping Statements for Social Anxiety

In social settings, Johnny felt very awkward. He did not enjoy the limelight or any attention focused on him at all!

"Dude," Johnny's buddies would say. "When are you going to get over this fear of talking to a woman?" Johnny would laugh off their comments.

Social Anxiety – Dreading, fearing, and/or expecting to be rejected and/or humiliated by others in social settings.

* A feeling of discomfort, fear, dread, or worry that is centered on our interactions with other people.
* Fear of being judged negatively by others.
* Fear of being evaluated negatively by others.

Is there hope for those that have social anxiety? Yes. EFT Tapping. Tap the statements that Johnny tapped to overcome his social anxiety.

80 EFT Tapping Statements for Adult Children of Alcoholics

Did you have a parent that was an alcoholic? Do you have difficulty relating and connecting to others? Do you have a strong need to be perfect? Is your self-esteem low and judge yourself harshly? Do you have a fear of abandonment and rejection? If so, then EFT Tapping might help.

Rebecca had lost her 4th job. She was defensive, argumentative, and resentful. Rebecca knew her boss was right in firing her.

Rebecca's childhood was anything but idyllic. Her father was a raging alcoholic. She was terrified of his anger. Rebecca tried to be perfect so her dad couldn't find fault with her. Home life was hell. She had to grow up really fast and was never allow to be a kid or to play.

Rebecca did see an EFT Practitioner and was able to heal the anger, the need to be perfect, and other issues one has when they have an alcoholic parent.

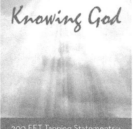

200 EFT Tapping Statements for Knowing God

So many questions surround this topic, God. Does God exist or is God a fabrication? Is God for real or just a concept? If God does exist, then what is God's role in our lives?

Do our prayers get answered or are we praying in vain? Does God make mistakes? God created Lucifer and then kicked out a third of his angels from heaven along with Lucifer. Was Lucifer a mistake and all the angels that choose to follow Lucifer? Do we just want to believe that a supreme being really cares about us, gave us our lives' purpose, a mission, and a destiny? God is as varied as there are people.

Many have said that God gave humans the power of choice and free will. If this is true, the consequences of our actions are ours alone. Yet, there are those who believe that God could intervene. God should take action to protect and provide for us.

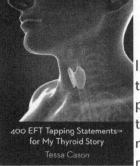

400 ET Tapping Statements for My Thyroid Story

In 2005, I was diagnosed with thyroid cancer. I researched the potential cause and discovered that 20 years after exposure to natural gas, thyroid issues will result. 20 years previous to the diagnosis, I lived in a townhouse for 850 days that had a gas leak.

While pursuing healing modalities after the exposure to natural gas, I began to realize that about 50% of our health issues are emotionally produced. The other 50% are the result of environmental factors such as smoking, chemicals, accidents, and/or hereditary.

I did not believe my emotional issues caused the thyroid cancer. It was the result of an environmental factor outside myself. BUT, since the thyroid was affected, if I worked on the emotional issues that had to do with the thyroid, it should impact the thyroid cancer. That was my theory.

100 EFT Tapping Statements for Fear of Computers

Can you image strapping on your Jet pack to get to work? Traveling on the Hyperloop that travels at speeds up to 600 mph to visit a friend that lives in another state? Stepping into your self-driving car that chauffeurs you to the restaurant? Soon all of these will be a part of our lives.

Modern technology! Most everyone knows that the computer can answer most any question. Most every job today and jobs of the future require at least some knowledge of computers.

Grandmere was intimidated by the computer. Her motivation was her granddaughter would was moving to another country. Granddaughter wants her to learn to use the computer so they can Skype when she is out of the country. Read how Grandmere was able to overcome her anxiety and fear of the computer.

200 EFT Tapping Statements for Sex

Is sex about the act or is sex about the intimacy shared by the act? Is sex about the orgasms or is it about the connection, touching, and cuddling?

In most culture, sex/lovemaking/intercourse is not discussed, explored, or a polite topic of conversation. For a fulfilling and satisfying sexual relationship, communication is important, yet many couples find it difficult to talk about sex.

Can you talk to your partner about sex?
Are you comfortable with your sexuality?
Do you know your partner's sexual strategy?

Our attitude, beliefs, and emotions determine our thoughts and feeling about sex. Dysfunctional beliefs can interfere with a healthy, fulfilling, satisfying sexual relationship. If we want to make changes in our lives, we have to recognize, acknowledge, and take ownership of our dysfunctional beliefs and emotions.

200 EFT Tapping Statements for Positive Thinking vs Positive Avoidance

If we keep piling more Band-Aids over a wound, the wound is still there. At some point, the wound needs to be examined, cleaned, and treated in order for heal.

Sometimes it is just "easier" to think positive when we really don't want to look at an issue. Positive Avoidance is denying the truth of a situation. It is a denial of our experience and our feelings about the situation.

When we try to push down our negative emotions, it is like trying to push a ball underwater. The ball pops back up.

Positive Thinking is the act of thinking good or affirmative thoughts, finding the silver lining around a dark cloud, and looking on the more favorable side of an event or condition. It is not denial, avoidance, or false optimism.

Books and Kindles eBooks by Tessa Cason

80 EFT TAPPING STATEMENTS FOR:
Abandonment
Abundance, Wealth, Money
Addictions
Adult Children of Alcoholics
Anger and Frustration
Anxiety and Worry
Change
"Less Than" and Anxiety
Manifesting a Romantic Relationship
Relationship with Self
Self Esteem
Social Anxiety
Weight and Emotional Eating

100 EFT Tapping Statements for Accepting Our Uniqueness and Being Different
100 EFT Tapping Statements for Being Extraordinary!
100 EFT Tapping Statements for Fear of Computers
100 EFT Tapping Statements for Feeling Deserving
100 EFT Tapping Statements for Feeling Fulfilled
200 EFT Tapping Statements for Conflict
200 EFT Tapping Statements for Healing a Broken Heart
200 EFT Tapping Statements for Knowing God
200 EFT Tapping Statements for Positive Thinking vs Positive Avoidance
200 EFT Tapping Statements for Procrastination
200 EFT Tapping Statements for PTSD
200 EFT Tapping Statements for Sex
200 EFT Tapping Statements for Wealth
240 EFT Tapping Statements for Fear
300 EFT Tapping Statements for Healing the Self
300 EFT Tapping Statements for Dealing with Obnoxious People
300 EFT Tapping Statements for Intuition
300 EFT Tapping Statements for Self-defeating Behaviors, Victim, Self-pity
340 EFT Tapping Statements for Healing From the Loss of a Loved One
400 EFT Tapping Statements for Being a Champion
400 EFT Tapping Statements for Being Empowered and Successful
400 EFT Tapping Statements for Dealing with Emotions
400 EFT Tapping Statements for Dreams to Reality
400 EFT Tapping Statements for My Thyroid Story

500 EFT Tapping Statements for Moving Out of Survival
700 EFT Tapping Statements for Weight, Emotional Eating, and Food Cravings
All Things EFT Tapping Manual
Emotional Significance of Human Body Parts
Muscle Testing – Obstacles and Helpful Hints

EFT TAPPING STATEMENTS FOR:
A Broken Heart, Abandonment, Anger, Depression, Grief, Emotional Healing
Anxiety, Fear, Anger, Self Pity, Change
Champion, Success, Personal Power, Self Confidence, Leader/Role Model
Prosperity, Survival, Courage, Personal Power, Success
PTSD, Disempowered, Survival, Fear, Anger
Weight & Food Cravings, Anger, Grief, Not Good Enough, Failure

OTHER BOOKS
Why we Crave What We Crave: The Archetypes of Food Cravings
How to Heal Our Food Cravings

EFT WORKBOOK AND JOURNAL FOR EVERYONE:
Abandonment
Abundance, Money, Prosperity
Addictions
Adult Children of Alcoholics
Anger, Apathy, Guilt
Anxiety/Worry
Being A Man
Being, Doing, Belonging
Champion
Change
Conflict
Courage
Dark Forces
Decision Making
Depression
Difficult/Toxic Parents
Difficult/Toxic People
Emotional Healing

Fear
Forgiveness
God
Grief
Happiness/Joy
Intuition
Leadership
Live Your Dreams
Life Purpose/Mission
People Pleaser
Perfectionism
Personal Power
Relationship w/Others
Relationship w/Self & Commitment to Self
Self Confidence
Self Worth/Esteem
Sex
Shame
Stress
Success
Survival
Transitions
Trust/Discernment
Victim, Self-pity, Self-Defeating Behavior, Shadow Self
Weight and Emotional Eating

Made in the USA
Las Vegas, NV
16 February 2023

67623559R00057